"Gut-wrenchingly honest, crammed with hope, warm and never preachy, this book is quite wonderful. Grace seeps through every page. Catherine offers vital help for all who navigate their way through pain – that means all of us. If you buy just one book this year, choose this one."

– *Jeff Lucas*, *author, speaker, broadcaster*

"Catherine Campbell is a living example of the old idea of an Irish 'saint and scholar'. Her words drip like honey from the comb. This book won't just encourage you, it will nurture you and sweeten your spirit. Don't just read the words, eat them and let them change your heart."

– *Malcolm Duncan*, *speaker, pastor of Gold Hill Baptist Church, and author of* Risk Takers

By the same author

God Knows Your Name
Broken Works Best
Rainbows for Rainy Days

UNDER THE RAINBOW

A mother's experiences of
the promises of God

Catherine Campbell

Every Blessing
Catherine Campbell
Isaiah 43:2

MONARCH
BOOKS

Oxford, UK & Grand Rapids, Michigan, USA

Published by Monarch Books
an imprint of
Lion Hudson plc
Wilkinson House, Jordan Hill Road,
Oxford OX2 8DR, England
Email: monarch@lionhudson.com
www.lionhudson.com/monarch

ISBN 978 0 85721 445 4
e-ISBN 978 0 85721 463 8

This edition 2013

Acknowledgments
Unless otherwise stated, Scripture quotations taken from the New King James Version. Copyright © 1982 by Thomas Nelson, Inc. Used by permission. All rights reserved. Scripture quotation marked NIV taken from the Holy Bible, New International Version Anglicised. Copyright © 1979, 1984, 2011 Biblica, formerly International Bible Society. Used by permission of Hodder & Stoughton Ltd, an Hachette UK company. All rights reserved. "NIV" is a registered trademark of Biblica. UK trademark number 1448790.

Extract pages 152–153 quoted from "We are the reason" by David Meece. Copyright © 1980 Meece Music. Admin by WORD Music and Song Solutions. Used with permission.

Every effort has been made to trace the original copyright holders where required. In some cases this has proved impossible. We shall be happy to correct any such omissions in future editions.

A catalogue record for this book is available from the British Library

Printed and bound in the UK, June 2013, LH26

Dedicated to

the memory of Cheryl and Joy, who continue
to bless my life every day.
Also to my husband Philip and son Paul,
whose love and support are my constant
strength;
and to Susie, who is teaching me once more
the delights of daughters.

With special thanks to

Mrs Lillian Hill and the staff of Hillcroft School, Dr E. Hicks, and the staff of Paul Ward and other departments of the Royal Belfast Hospital for Sick Children, for your care of Cheryl and Joy over many years.

Always remember that *you* made a difference.

I am leading my child to the heavenly land
I am guiding her day by day
And I ask her now, as I take her hand
To come home by a rugged way.
It's not the way she herself would choose
For its beauty she cannot see,
But she knows not what her soul would lose
If she trod not that path with me!

Author unknown

Contents

Author's Note

When I wrote the original version of *Under the Rainbow* back in 2008 I had no idea of the impact it would have on so many lives. To say it has been humbling would be an understatement. Sharing the years I had with our profoundly disabled daughters in an open and frank manner was not easy to do. Once the affairs of my heart, both emotional and spiritual, were seen in print, I could not take them back. I didn't realize then how vulnerable it would make me feel when I recognized that thousands of people would hold my heart in their hands.

However, the other side of exposing my inner wounds to all and sundry was the freedom it gave me to share how God worked in my pain, and also through the lives of our two remarkable little girls. In turn, that gave many readers the opportunity to share their own difficult situations with others and sometimes with me. Communications of all types have come my way over the years, explaining how this little book has touched lives, and confirming the step of faith I took in writing it.

Unfortunately, there was little opportunity for the book to be seen beyond Northern Ireland, and when the original publishers went out of business in 2010 it was no longer available anywhere. Saddened, I found it hard to accept that it had accomplished all that God had for it to do, but my hands were tied. It was simply out of print… until now.

My current publisher, Monarch, has given me the amazing privilege of revisiting, revising and expanding *Under the Rainbow*. If you have come to it again, the story is the same but with some new material that was not included in the first edition. If you have read *Broken Works Best* (Monarch, 2012) you may recognize some of the events that I used there to illustrate the teaching on how "God turns our pain into gain". However, *Under the Rainbow* is a different book. It is simply the story of one young mother who discovered that in the storms of life God allows us to stand under the rainbow of His promises: promises that He always keeps.

What is especially exciting for me is that the message of *Under the Rainbow* will now be given the opportunity to reach far beyond the shores of the Emerald Isle. My prayer is that wherever it goes it will bring God's grace into the lives of those who have been rocked by difficulty and disappointment.

My heartfelt thanks go to Tony Collins and the team at Monarch for making this possible. Thanks also go to my ever-patient proofreaders, my friend Liz Young and my husband Philip, my greatest encourager.

So whether you have launched into *Under the Rainbow* for the first time or the second time, I place my heart in your hands, remembering what God frequently whispers in my ear: "… the things which happened to me have actually turned out for the furtherance of the gospel" (Philippians 1:12). For that I bring Him praise.

Prologue

The changing room was unusually quiet that Sunday afternoon when I arrived for my shift. A quick glance at my watch confirmed that I wasn't late. Missing lunch may have made my tummy grumble but it ensured that I had plenty of time to change into my uniform. The absence of fellow nurses meant one of two things: either the hospital wasn't too busy or it was very short-staffed. I hoped the former was true as I headed down to the end of the main corridor where the Sick Baby Unit was housed.

Working with the babies was a delight, especially as the unit cared for babies of normal gestation, who usually needed only a few days of extra care before they were reunited with their mothers. It was the kind of work that set the old maternal instinct in motion. How different and much less stressful it was than working with the very tiny babies of the Premature Baby Unit, whose treatment was critical and life saving.

There was a lift in my step and a song in my heart as I pushed open the huge old oak door into the unit. Church had been particularly uplifting that morning, and everything in the world was good.

"Nurse, come with me!"

The words brought me sharply to attention as I looked over my shoulder to see if the command was really directed at me. The brusque, even angry manner of the midwife in charge sent my brain into overdrive.

Surely I wasn't late? What had I done wrong? The usually pleasant atmosphere of the unit was ice cold. No friendly hellos from the other staff, each obviously trying to get on with their own business. Only the occasional cry of a baby dared to break the silence.

I followed her meekly to a cubicle positioned right at the back of the ward. It was normally only used for babies with some kind of infectious illness: babies who needed to be nursed in strict isolation. I had never seen it used during my time in the unit. In fact I had never even seen the light on in it before.

As we entered the bleak room, a sudden movement underneath a pink baby blanket made me jump, an audible gasp escaping before I could stop it.

"This is Barbara," the midwife announced, ignoring my evident horror. "Born three hours ago, weighing nine pounds. Apgar score – low."

I was annoyed at displaying such obvious shock at the sight before me, especially as the midwife continued, "As you can see, this little one was born with gross hydrocephalus and spina bifida."

Not even her years of experience could hide how difficult this speech was for her to make.

"Your job is to look after Barbara until she dies. It shouldn't take long," she continued, "the surgeons can't help. It's just a matter of time. Her mother won't be visiting. She's much too upset. She just wants us to tell her when it's all over."

She went on to give me staccato instructions as to how I was to care for this pathetic little specimen of humanity. I could see now why she was cross, and why the unit was already mourning for the living dead. Barbara's head was not just big with the build-up of fluid around her brain, it was huge, making her features look squashed and even, dare I say it, ugly. The open lesion on her spine was raw and seeping. Spinal fluid was trying to escape from the open wound, now covered by a dressing. Her two paralysed little legs lay limp, as if they didn't belong to the rest of her body.

Instructions over, the midwife looked at me with what seemed like accusatory disdain in her eyes.

"You're a Christian, aren't you?" she snapped. "How can you believe in a God who allows children to be born like that?"

Her words delivered what felt like a slap in the face. She turned and left the room quickly, and her disappearance was welcome, because in that instant I could not answer her question. I just didn't know why.

As I leaned over the cot I couldn't stop a tear falling onto Barbara's face. As I quickly brushed it off with my fingers, she rooted, just like any other baby looking for its mother's breast. She stretched her little arms, showing me all her tiny fingers, and started to cry.

"Feed her," the midwife had said. "She'll probably bring it all up again, but the sucking will bring her comfort."

Two minutes later Barbara was in my arms sucking away at a bottle of formula for dear life. Where on earth this very sick baby got such a strong suck from I don't know, but when she opened her big blue eyes as she finished her feed she stole the heart of this young student midwife.

"You are not ugly, baby, you are beautiful," I whispered in her ear. "God put me here with you for this little while so that I could love you until He takes you home."

The day was very difficult, consisting of a constant round of feeding and cleaning up, and of trying to make Barbara as comfortable as possible. Her heavy head was uncomfortable to hold, but I counted it a privilege to care for her, and as I left at the end of my shift I committed her to God, believing she would die overnight.

Philip was waiting outside in the car to take me home at the end of a long day. As I belted up, the pain of the day overwhelmed me, and in a gush of emotions and words I poured out my heart to my totally unprepared husband.

"Why does God allow babies to be born like Barbara? What has she ever done to deserve it? Surely the midwife was right to be angry with God? She's so bad, her own mother can't even bear to look at her! It's just not fair!"

Long into the night we tried to make sense of the theology of suffering. All the usual Scripture verses seemed weak and unconvincing in the light of the baby that I'd held in my arms that day. The fact that God is sovereign, or the truth that God's ways are not our ways (see Isaiah 55:8), did not easily drop from knowledge to understanding. My heart seemed very far from my head as I tried to sleep.

When I arrived for work the next day I was amazed at the sight of night staff in the cubicle at the end of the ward. It could only mean one thing: Barbara had made it through the night! For the next five days we were together all of my working hours. In those precious days I would sing to her of Heaven, and tell her of the wonderful Saviour who would be waiting for her. And even if she hadn't a clue what I was talking about, I went ahead and told her about the glorious new body she would receive. There were times I felt we were visited by Heaven in that room, especially as I rocked her when she was distressed. Peace would descend, and in those moments I knew God loved her, even if I couldn't work out the theology.

The following Saturday my shift started at noon.

"Quick! Hold Barbara while I change her sheet. Her mother has changed her mind and wants to see her, but she's going fast. I hope they make it in time."

The midwife carefully placed Barbara in my arms, and as I kissed her forehead I knew she really was dying this time. Before the sheet was tucked into the small cot, Barbara was in the place I had sung to her about so often on the previous days. She was so brave. So beautiful. And now – so perfect.

Unfortunately her mother only ever held her after she had died.

Later, when the family left that sad little room, the midwife explained that they never let a baby go to the morgue accompanied only by porters. The last act of care for any dead baby was for the little one to be carried from the unit by a member of the nursing staff. Her tone was now very different to that of the previous Sunday, as she had watched me care for Barbara all week.

"I think it's too much to ask of a student midwife," she said, "but it should be for you to decide. I will go if you prefer."

There was no decision to make. It would be my last demonstration of love for this brave little girl.

I sat in the passenger seat of the porter's van as we crossed the large hospital site to the morgue. Barbara was all wrapped up in my arms, just as if she was sleeping. There was no conversation. I wondered if maybe the porter was a daddy, and this would undoubtedly be the worst job he would have to do that day. The mortuary attendant was waiting for us, his hand holding open a large door.

"Middle shelf," he said, with no apparent hint of feeling. "Take your blanket back with you."

"Oh, no," I replied quickly, as I carefully placed her

deformed little body on the metal shelf, "it's much too cold in here."

Neither man responded to the foolish suggestion of the young nurse. Perhaps it didn't sound so foolish after all, as the door clanked shut.

Back in the unit I threw myself into the busyness of my work, my life forever touched by the six-day struggle of one little girl. As I settled down to sleep that night I gently stroked my tummy. "Well, little one, at least I know *you* will never be born like Barbara. God will take care of you. Your mummy and daddy love God and He would never let anything bad happen to you. Of that I am sure."

1

Cheryl

❝ What's this? Are we going home the long way?"
I asked, as our bright orange Volkswagen beetle
turned left out of the church car park instead of right.

"I think it's about time we showed this baby who is
boss!" my husband chuckled. "Perhaps a long walk will
help the little miss or master to make a speedier entrance."

Philip, usually much more patient than I, had started
to tire of hearing those annoying words: "No sign of that
baby yet?" As if we could do anything about it! Besides
which, our own excitement was also hard to contain.
This welcome addition to our lives couldn't come soon
enough, especially as my due date had already passed
one week earlier.

The Antrim coast road looked particularly beautiful
that evening. The sun was still high and the clear blue
sky merged seamlessly into the glassy sea, obscuring
the distant horizon. The sight of sailing boats moving on
the water was a surprising treat, as there didn't appear
to be even a breeze. The drive was lovely and our time
together was intimate as we shared the inmost things of
our hearts. Soon our lives would change with the arrival
of a longed-for baby. For this little time left we could enjoy
each other's company undisturbed.

We walked far into the forest before an alarming
thought hit me. What if this long walk *did* have the desired

effect? What if I went into labour here? How would Philip get me back to the car, never mind the extra miles to the hospital? I don't know if it was the descending chill in the air, or the slight concern about being in the wrong place at the wrong time that turned us back to the car, but turn we did and home we headed. The long walk in the beautiful forest proved enjoyable, but nothing more, and as we retired for the night our precious bundle was still secure in her comfortable hidey-hole. Sleep came easily as we rested happy in the knowledge that our lives and our baby were in the centre of God's will. After all, not a day had passed but we had placed both into the Lord's hands.

Our next car journey together was only two days later. The scenery on the way was completely different from the beautiful coast road. This time we travelled through a rather bleak and battered Belfast, in the days when armed soldiers still patrolled our streets. The maternity hospital was on the then infamous Falls Road, and while many still feared that notorious area, I was used to its environs, having worked at the "Royal" site since I was only seventeen.

Anyway, I was just glad that at last the obstetrician had decided to intervene, as this baby was oblivious to the fact that she was keeping a lot of people waiting! Philip was entering the unknown. I, on the other hand, as a now-qualified midwife, knew exactly what lay ahead. I sometimes wonder who was better off.

After seven and a half hours' labour, on 2 August 1979 at 1.26 a.m., a small dark-haired midwife announced in her broad Scottish accent: "It's a little lassie! You have a bonnie wee daughter!"

Our hearts seemed to explode with joy as our little girl was lifted into the air for us to catch our first glimpse.

As I held her close, my heart flooded with praise to the Saviour who had brought such happiness into our lives.

A couple of minutes later she was handed over to Philip, all wrapped up in a warm green towel, her little face wrinkled and her hair still matted. Surely there could not have been a more beautiful sight as she lay quietly in her proud daddy's arms with her tiny, still-blue hands clasped under her chin.

Trying out her name for the first time, Philip softly kissed her cheek.

"Cheryl," he whispered, "it suits you so well, for you are surely our little 'darling'."

If ever a man looked besotted by a baby, it was that man, that day!

By 3 a.m., with Daddy packed off home, Cheryl and I settled down for a short but peaceful sleep after our tiring labour experience. As I looked across the room I could hardly believe she was mine. The little kicks I had felt for the past months now had a face, and for sure my life would never be the same again. Never before had I felt so complete. Drifting off to sleep I was oblivious to what lay ahead.

Those days in hospital were a lovely time of "getting-to-know-you" that preceded a wonderful homecoming. The flat appeared brighter than usual that day, and a large bouquet of summer flowers filled the room with their fresh fragrance. It was Granny's way of welcoming home her own daughter and her first grandchild. The fuss that one tiny little baby could bring to a home was enormous, and we were only too pleased to involve all the family. Presents seemed to flood in, and I felt that Cheryl must surely have the biggest wardrobe in Ulster, incorporating every frill and flounce imaginable. The hallway to our flat constantly echoed to the sound of happy conversation as night after night friends made their way to welcome the most beautiful addition to our family.

What is it about a newborn baby that creates such emotion? Perhaps it is the sight of perfection in miniature: the tiny toes and fingers displaying even smaller nails; the little pug nose shadowing the sweetest of rosebud lips; too much wrinkled skin, so soft that you can't stop yourself from caressing it. Or maybe it is the matchless expressions of innocence that cross her beautiful face as she sleeps, yawns, or stretches in readiness for another feed. Maybe the smell of baby powder mixed with their utter dependence on you for their every need acts as some kind of a catalyst deep within your being. I don't know. I only know that she brought out something in me that I could never have imagined, and am not eloquent enough to describe.

The huge privilege of delivering around forty babies had been a tremendous experience, mixing anxiety, skill and sheer delight. To participate in such a special moment in the lives of others was indeed precious – yet it paled into insignificance when compared to having this one baby of my own.

In a moment of time she had captured my heart.

My midwifery experience allowed me to avoid many of the concerns of a new mother. Handling Cheryl for whatever reason, be it bathing, dressing or feeding, was never fraught with anxiety. It was pure delight. And so I quickly relaxed into the role of motherhood. Or so I thought.

Cheryl being an August baby allowed us to enjoy sunny days and long summer evenings. They were the perfect opportunity for getting out the rather large and grand pram for leisurely walks, and for showing baby off. On one such day I decided Cheryl and I would walk the mile or so to our local bank to open a savings account for her, as people had been so generous with their gifts. Cheryl had just finished feeding and I knew we would have plenty of time to get there and back before she woke up. So up the long hilly road we headed on a beautiful sunny afternoon. Cheryl was still sleeping when we reached the bank, and I parked her pram right outside the door and joined the long queue.

The time passed fairly quickly as I chatted with some of the people I knew. After handing over the completed form and money, I placed the new savings passbook into my handbag and set off for home. The return journey was all the quicker because it was downhill. Then, as I put my hand on the door of the entrance hallway, I suddenly identified the nagging little doubt that had bothered me all the way home.

I had left the baby outside the bank!

Sheer panic engulfed me as I turned on my heel to run all the way back. All kinds of thoughts rushed across my mind. How could I have been so stupid? Would she still be there? Maybe someone had kidnapped her. Or she might be crying and someone would have called the police. Social services would take her away from me. I wasn't fit to be a mother! Why, oh why, did Philip have to be out? The car could get me there quicker.

By this time sweat was mingled with my tears as I sobbed in time with my frantic paces. Only once had I been called upon to make up the cross-country team in school, but on this day I think I could have been picked for the Olympics! What a sight I must have looked and sounded: by the time I reached the half-way point I was wheezing like the asthmatic I was. Barely able to take another breath, there was no time to stop to look for a hankie or an inhaler.

"Please, God, please let her be safe!" I cried, all the way to the bank.

Before crossing the road at the shops I could see her brown pram in the distance, but it brought me no comfort. What if the pram were empty? How could I tell Philip I had left his little daughter all on her own among strangers? I was a sobbing mess, bumping into people as I tried one last sprint to reach the pram. Momentarily, I was afraid to look inside, but in an instant the fear was replaced by relief.

Cheryl was still fast asleep.

Our beautiful little daughter was totally unaware of the dreadful mistake her mother had just made. With a very wet hankie in one hand and holding tightly to my precious cargo with the other I made my way home yet again... exhausted.

It was an important lesson in the folly of over-confidence, and a realization that this little one was going to need more than me to look out for her.

"Thank you, God."

2

"Never Normal"

Cheryl was such a good baby.

She fed and slept right on cue, and apart from a few hours of pacing up and down with her through colic each evening, those early months were sheer joy. Blonde shoots started to appear from her baldy little head. Smiling came just a little later than the expected six weeks, but, boy, was it worth waiting for! Her blue eyes sparkled with the rise of the corners of her rosebud lips. Visits to the grandparents were always a treat for all of us. Weekly weight and length gains were discussed, as was whatever beautiful fashion item was worn on that particular day. The first Christmas passed with flash photography in abundance, and even the winter did not seem so miserable that year.

That was until Granny Fraser lowered her voice one day, and with words she obviously did not want to use, said: "Catherine, do you not think Cheryl should be able to hold her head up a bit better by now? She doesn't seem to be reaching for anything."

I was silenced and shocked at the implied suggestion, but before I had time to respond, my mother continued with her rehearsed speech.

"I think she should be showing a wee bit more progress by now, love, she is nearly five months old."

My shock turned to rage as I grabbed the sleeping child out of her doting granny's arms.

"How dare you say that Cheryl is slow," I retorted angrily. "I'm the midwife here, you know! All babies progress at different speeds. She's just a typical wee girl. Quiet and gentle. There's absolutely nothing wrong with her!"

Granny's tears did nothing to assuage my anger that she could possibly imagine that there could be anything wrong with my baby. After that she held her peace, and with Cheryl all tucked up in her pram I quickly made my exit, determined never to give any more thought to the concerns of one who had seen three of her own safely through childhood.

But the question would not go away, no matter how much I tried to put it out of my mind. It plagued my every waking moment; kept me up at night; cast a shadow over my soul.

When I was fourteen years old I had made an amazing discovery. Having watched a school classmate change almost overnight from being a rude, obnoxious character to a genuinely warm and kind girl, I was curious. I had always been the one who never missed church, the one who was quiet and thoughtful, yet this girl talked about knowing Jesus as Saviour in a way I had never heard before.

The lurking question of "what is a real Christian?" was answered one evening when I attended a youth meeting with this girl. Other teenagers used phrases that night that I had not been aware of before, phrases like "born again"; "trusting in Christ"; "being saved". I did not understand what it all meant, but I did see something real in their lives that I wanted for myself. They looked happy and satisfied. They seemed to know where they were going in life, and I wanted to head in the same direction.

"So being a Christian isn't just a matter of going to church?" I quizzed myself as I rushed home. "It's all about knowing Jesus for yourself. How on earth do you do that?"

One amazing fact about God is that He is true to His Word, even if we don't know it. As a seeking and rather confused teenager, I didn't know then that the Bible says in Jeremiah 29:13, "You will seek Me and find Me, when you search for Me with all your heart." But God knew it, and when I prayed that night for Him to show me how I could get to know Jesus, He showed me a picture of the Cross. For the first time ever I saw that Jesus had died for me, in order that I could get to know Him. All the churchgoing in the world couldn't make me a Christian. It was "Christ in" me that could make me a brand new person (see 2 Corinthians 5:17).

Once my younger sister was asleep, I quietly crept on to my knees at the side of my bed. I didn't know any fancy words, I only knew that my wrongdoing was what had sent Jesus to the Cross, so I asked Him to forgive me and to come and live in my life. There was no blinding light, no voice from Heaven, simply a deep sense that God had done what I had asked (see John 1:12).

It has always puzzled me that so many people expect the Christian life to be boring and restrictive. Nothing could be further from the truth. That night started a roller-coaster ride of excitement and deep joy that I wouldn't have swapped with any teenager who was doing all the "normal" things. I didn't need to drink or take drugs in order to have a good time, and I was always able to remember what I did the next day!

Eight years on I could look back and say that I had no regrets. Following Jesus was more than I had ever dreamed. Life was wonderful. The Bible was real and relevant to my everyday living. I had always believed God was in control, and that I could safely leave my life in His hands, but now, somewhere deep in the recesses of my heart, I could feel a little crack forming. It was being chiselled out by a fear that I didn't realize I had hidden away. And the fear had a face: Barbara's face.

Baby clinic was on Thursday. I determined to ask Janet, my health visitor and friend, if she would have a closer look at Cheryl. Her six-month assessment was almost due anyway. Then maybe Granny would believe me that Cheryl was as normal as any other little baby girl.

Over the weeks that followed, I fooled myself into believing that Janet's response – to schedule more health checks – was merely to dispel my concerns rather than to seek help. Even though we were passed from pillar to post, seeing a variety of doctors, I was convinced that each visit was a sensible rather than necessary consultation. I only remembered the reassuring comments.

"If it's OK with you, Catherine, I'd like a colleague of mine to carry out a formal assessment on Cheryl. As you know, I specialize mostly in neonates now. He's much more up to date with this sort of thing. He'll see you quickly, though – there's got to be some perks in the job," suggested the paediatrician.

He was someone I knew from midwifery training, and the rest of the conversation was taken up with chat about work. Surely this will be the last, and I can get on with the job of enjoying my first baby's first year, I thought, as we headed for home.

True to his word the appointment came quickly, although I was shocked by the content of the letter.

"Your child has been referred for assessment at the Child Development Clinic." I thought we were going to see a colleague, not a whole troop of people. The letter went on: "The assessment will last for two and a half hours, with half an hour allocated to each professional."

With eyes agog and jaw dropped I read on. Cheryl was to see a paediatrician, a physiotherapist, a speech therapist, an occupational therapist, and a social worker. She was barely seven months old. Why on earth did she need to see all these people?

It was a beautiful spring afternoon as we headed to the hospital. Philip had cleared his diary for the rest of the day and, ever the optimist, he was making reassuring noises as he took on the role of protector for the two ladies in his life. His little daughter might be a bit slow, was his assessment of the situation, but she would catch up – just wait and see. Meanwhile my heart felt as if I were betraying her, almost as if taking her to this place would change her into something she was not. I held her all the closer, with a determination deep inside that I was not going to leave this place without answers. I had had enough of uncertainty.

She looked so beautiful. Teething had put roses on her cheeks, and when she smiled her one tiny tooth looked like a badge of honour in the middle of a round little face. I was confident that she could not fail to impress in her pink frilly dress, yet as I looked at her tiny fingers tightly locked around mine I prayed: "Please, God, let everything be OK."

It was a tedious afternoon and I was disappointed that she was scheduled to see the doctor last. After all, he was the important one. The frilly dress was removed almost immediately as one by one the different therapists put Cheryl through her paces. Without the material trimmings she suddenly looked fragile in the hands of these strangers. My confidence was beginning to wane.

She was poked and prodded, and expected to do all kinds of things that, as far as I was concerned, were far too much for a child of seven months to master.

I answered dozens of questions, but, out of character, I asked very few. Cheryl behaved very well and I was so proud of her, but by the time we got to see the doctor she was fretful and tired.

"What a pity she couldn't have seen him earlier," I said to my weary husband, "she's just too exhausted to impress him now."

We were shown into a large room with windows on two sides, draped by long curtains with a bold rose print. There were toys strewn on a mat in the corner, and a large wooden tricycle that looked as if it had been made by hand. The room was dishevelled, witness to the fact that we were the last to be seen at the clinic that day.

The paediatrician was a tall, slim, grandfatherly figure of a man. When he smiled his eyes sparkled, and the surrounding laughter lines gave away his friendly nature and put us at our ease.

"So this is Cheryl," he said gently as he lifted her out of my arms. "You have had a busy day, little one, it's no wonder you are feeling a bit sad."

I watched with amazement as he totally ignored us and took our tear-stained little girl on a walk around the room. He tenderly kissed her forehead and talked to her cheek to cheek in hushed tones. The calming melody of his voice stopped her crying, and the secure hold he had on her gave both her and us the assurance that she was safe in his arms.

Here is a man who clearly has a lifetime of experience

with children, I thought. He loves them, and they love him. He held her for nearly the whole time we were with him, every now and then rocking her when she showed any sign of unrest. Apart from that he did nothing else with her. There were questions for us, of course, as he flicked through the rest of the reports from the previous assessors.

"You can dress her now," he said as he put her back into my arms. "The physio has asked for hip X-rays, and you can have that done before you go home today. She will be in contact soon to arrange an appointment at the physio department. See you in six months' time."

X-rays, physio, appointments?

"Is there a problem?" I asked, plucking up the courage to take the bull by the horns. "I mean… her development is just a bit slow. She will catch up, won't she?"

As the words tripped and tumbled out of my mouth, the doctor leaned forward in amazement as if I had just uttered the most ridiculous question he had ever heard.

I braced myself for his answer as this kindly gentleman seemed to undergo a kind of metamorphosis, suddenly towering over us; his voice changed into a clarion of doom. The words he uttered crashed in on us like a verbal baseball bat, wreaking havoc on our lives.

"Mrs Campbell," he said incredulously, "don't you realize? Your little girl is severely handicapped. She won't catch up. She will never be normal."

I gasped in disbelief and shock. The doctor's words had become fingers choking my breath; my head was spinning, my heart was thumping and I was trying, with little success, to hold back a flood of tears. He was still talking, but his voice was far away as if he was in another room… something about us having seen three doctors. Did none of them tell us that Cheryl had microcephaly?

"Her brain hasn't grown properly," he was saying, "and that's why she has such a small head."

Faster than lightning, my life was falling apart in front of me. "Never be normal" was all I could hear, and I was sure if we could only get away from this man everything would go back to the way it was before we entered this awful place.

"Never be normal" thundered in my head in time to the thumping of my heart. The panic and need to escape reached a climax. I had to get out of that room! The doctor was still talking as I made for the door; this time he was apologizing that we had to receive such bad news in this way.

The silence in the car was broken only by my stifled sobs. My brain was in overdrive trying to process all the information we had received in the past few months. How could they not have told me? Why didn't I ask more questions along the way? Everyone who had seen her was always measuring her head. Why was I only picking up on that now? Ever since Barbara I had been on the lookout for the big head, the sign of hydrocephalus, and when I first set eyes on my darling daughter I was so pleased that hers was small and dainty. How could I have missed it?

"'Never be normal', he said. How can we tell our parents that their first, beautiful grandchild will 'never be normal'?"

I didn't realize that my last thoughts were spoken aloud until Philip's reply interrupted them.

"He could be wrong, Catherine. She's only a bit slow and we'll work hard with her. She will catch up, just you wait and see." When I didn't reply, he added, "God will make it all right."

Then I caught a glimpse of his face in the rear-view mirror. My poor Philip, my dear, dear, husband. His eyes portrayed a look of deep pain and helplessness. He had no idea how, as the head of this family, he could fix the disaster that had arrived on his lap. Daddies were meant to be able to fix anything. Husbands were meant to be the protectors of their wives. At least, that was what all the good parenting books had said. Now, in this moment, denial was the best thing he could come up with, and I loved him even for that.

How could it all go so horribly wrong? How could we leave our beautiful happy home one lunchtime and return at teatime with our lives completely turned upside down? How could we go out with a few concerns about our firstborn and return with a different child? A child for whom there would be none of the usual guarantees, except one.

"She will never be normal."

We had moved from the sunshine of a trouble-free life to the darkness of the fiercest storm, as if we had been dropped over a cliff, and there was no rescue in sight.

The family were heartbroken, but they jumped right in to support and love us even more than before. Cheryl, on the other hand, was totally oblivious to all that was going on around her. Hot tears splashing on to her cheeks at regular intervals only brought a smile. She wasn't a different child; rather, she was exactly the same beautiful, blue-eyed blonde that we had come to know and love for the previous seven months. Even my anger at not knowing sooner was cooled by the fact that we had been given all that time to get to know her before the bombshell was dropped. For that I will forever be grateful.

Bad news travels fast.

In no time at all our friendly neighbourhood and church family were in a state of shock. It was almost as if a death had taken place, and everyone was in mourning.

Thoughtful whispers and caring glances followed us wherever we went. Our sad news might have been the talk of the neighbourhood but I knew it wasn't merely gossip, but sympathy: "Such a lovely young couple to be burdened with such sad news" was something I overheard on more than one occasion.

The hallway to our flat was once again busy night after night as people made their little pilgrimages to see us. This time joyful laughter was replaced by hushed tones. For some a hug and tears were enough to assure us of their love, while others felt a need to leave a verse of Scripture with us to convince us of God's love. Very soon, however, this began to grate on me, as my broken heart could no more understand what God was doing than any of these friends could understand what I was going through. As soon as a Bible was opened I felt as if I had been stood in front of a firing squad, with verses hitting me with the speed of a machine gun. If one more person had said, "All things work together for good to those who love God, to those who are the called according to His purpose" (Romans 8:28), I think I would have hit them! It was a real lesson to me in how and when to quote Scripture at people.

But somehow when *God* whispers His Word to your heart, that's a completely different matter.

From early on we are conditioned to wear masks, especially in the Christian church. Fear of not living up to others' expectations, alongside a genuine wish not to let the Lord down, tricks us into showing people what we think they want to see. For me that meant I should put on my smile with my Sunday go-to-meeting clothes, and respond with the words "I'm fine" when people asked, "How are you?" After all, my husband was a preacher and it wouldn't do for people to see his wife fall apart, or to hear the anguish of her heart as she pleaded with God every day for a miracle.

Few knew of the nights I cried myself to sleep, and I often even kept those tears for the nights Philip was away on business for the Lord as an evangelist. As far as I was concerned, Cheryl's diagnosis could not possibly be in God's will for our lives. In those early days after that damning diagnosis I had never felt so emotionally out of control, or so unsure of God's love or purposes. Consequently I would cover my head with the duvet and cry out to God every night.

"God! I don't know what you're doing with my life. None of this makes any sense. Please help me!"

On one such evening, Philip was away in England working with a church, and Cheryl was fast asleep. Curled up in my usual position, I was weeping and praying, going through the same old questions of pain and misery. But it was far from any usual night, because on that particular night God crept into my room, and He Himself whispered His Word to my aching heart. The words that He used had been hidden deep in my heart from shortly after I became a Christian. They were words that blew me away, because then, as a young Christian, I had thought: "With a God like this you could change the world." And in the darkness of that room and of my soul, He reminded me of the promise I had read years before.

"Catherine," He said as clearly as if He had been sitting beside me. "Fear not… you are Mine. When you pass through the waters, I will be with you; and through the rivers, they shall not overflow you. When you walk through the fire you shall not be burned… for I am the Lord your God"(Isaiah 43:1–3).

I pulled the covers off my head, almost expecting to

see my Heavenly Father. His voice was so clear and for the first time in weeks I felt His presence binding up the pain in my heart. Peace flooded the room like the dawn dispelling the darkness. He did love me after all! With the sense of His presence as physical as the duvet that covered my tired body, I relished what God was speaking to my soul. I wasn't to be afraid, because the God of Heaven was assuring me that *I belonged to Him*. In all these "waters" of suffering He was promising to be right there with me. The journey that I had embarked upon was not one I had to walk alone. Every step was going to be marked with a promise… "I will be with you" (See Isaiah 43:2).

God's first rainbow to me was the promise of His presence… given right in the middle of my storm. In the same way that God had put a rainbow right in the thing that Noah feared most, the cloud, so God had placed His promise in the thing I feared most, the unknown future. God had not deserted me after all. The only niggle in my mind as I settled for sleep was the mention of *rivers* and *fire*. Surely that didn't mean there was more ahead?

Babies and early mornings are synonymous. But I didn't mind, as I couldn't wait to check out those whispered verses from the book of Isaiah. The sense of peace had remained through the night, and with tea in hand and Bible on knee, I searched the Scriptures for myself.

"How could I have got it so wrong?" I wondered. "Nowhere does God promise us a trouble-free life."

I moved from Isaiah to Job and read: "Man is born to trouble as the sparks fly upward" (Job 5:7) and on to Matthew 5:45 where Jesus says His Father "sends rain on the just and on the unjust". As I thought about these words I remembered a bookmark a friend had given me some time before. It talked about God not promising us the delights of skies ever blue, or joy without sorrow or peace without pain.

Why did I think that just because we loved God that nothing bad could ever happen to us? An avid reader, I had read many books about missionaries who had suffered greatly. If bad things had happened to these giants of the faith, what made me think there was some exemption clause written into my life? Sitting in the early light of the summer sun I sighed at the apparent ease with which we can fall into the devil's trap of the prosperity gospel, which preaches that if we follow Christ, everything will turn out our way. Then when the fake promise fails, we experience disappointment with God. And those of us who are disappointed with God are easily turned away from the narrow path.

As I finished my tea, I knew that God's promise was true. He would be with me, and I would never have to walk this journey alone. But I also knew something I had chosen to ignore until now: pain is part of the human package, even for the Christian. Cheryl was still disabled. As I closed my Bible I vowed I wouldn't stop praying for our sweet child. Maybe God would change His mind.

When Cheryl was around six months old I had returned to work for two nights a week in Coronary Care, rather than resuming my full-time hours in midwifery. This way I could have the best of both worlds: precious time with my daughter and a job that I found exciting, that also helped with the family finances.

Normally I got a lift home from work in the morning, but on this particular day I had to take the bus. Tiredness has a way of lowering your guard, and as I sat on the bus I was feeling exhausted and a bit sorry for myself. In addition, the bus was crawling at a snail's pace along the route, picking up passengers at every stop. Agitation was setting in when the bus stopped yet again, but I noticed the people in front of me adjusting their positions. A few of them moved to the aisle seat, while others shuffled uncomfortably, setting their bags or newspapers on the seats next to them.

I was puzzled.

The young man who had just boarded was chatting loudly to the driver as he purchased his ticket. He carried a large plastic lunchbox under his arm, and smiled broadly as he made his way down the aisle, shouting "Hello" to anyone who would take their eyes off the windows and look at him. His slightly slanted eyes, low-set ears and thickness of speech gave away the fact that he had Down's syndrome.

Suddenly it all made sense.

People shuffling around and moving their bags to block seats made it clear that no one wanted him to sit beside them. This young man was different, and the rejection of his difference made me feel ashamed. As he reached my seat I smiled at him and said "Hello." His face almost parted with the huge grin he made in response, and he walked straight to the back seat, where, my guess is, he sat every morning. And as handbags and newspapers were put back in place, my tears came.

"Maybe one day people will treat my little girl with the same disdain," I thought as I tried to compose myself. The picture of such blatant rejection forming in my mind was difficult to bear.

This random group of people on the bus had made one thing clear: "different" is not acceptable.

3

Designer Made?

The old adage "love is blind" has been used as an excuse throughout the centuries for people who refuse or are slow to see the faults in someone else, simply because of their love for them. We have all witnessed a marriage break-up, and been bewildered that *she didn't see it coming*. But then, she loved him… and "love is blind". We have listened on the news to some poor mother testify that *her son was a good boy*, when the evidence reveals him to be a murderer. But then, she loved him… and "love is blind". For seven months I was convinced that I had the most beautiful, normal daughter in the world. Other people, even my own mother, thought differently. But then, I loved her… and "love is blind".

How could I not have seen it? Just like the boy on the bus, Cheryl was different, yet I had refused to recognize it. Quite a number of our friends had babies in the same year as Cheryl was born. I foolishly thought how lovely it was that Cheryl was still such a cuddly baby, while these other babies wriggled and fussed at times when being held. Each one of my friends' children would strive for independence in the simplest of things, from holding their own feeding cup to reaching for a favourite toy. Cheryl, on the other hand, had always been the quiet, gentle little girl, who relished all the attention others gave to her. She never screamed in temper at something she couldn't reach. In fact, she never reached for anything.

And I didn't notice.

All her little baby friends had strong, big heads, while she had a dainty little one covered scantily with lovely blonde hair.

No problem, I thought, they are boys, after all.

In fact I was glad that her head was small, as she seemed to find it so hard to hold it up without help. When I went to lift one of my friends' children, they almost rose up to meet me. Cheryl, on the other hand, would have slipped through my hands like a rag doll if I hadn't held on to her tightly. Yet I had refused to let it register in my heart. Her hands were always tightly closed, yet she was unable to hold on to a toy by herself. She'll get the hang of it sometime, I told myself.

One thing she could do really well, though, was smile, and what a smile! The whole room lit up when Cheryl smiled, and when you tickled her knees she threw back her head and laughed, just like every other baby. And for some reason, this normally astute nurse was completely blind to the fact that her baby was different. In fact, my baby had major developmental problems. But then, I loved her… and "love is blind".

Cheryl's diagnosis of microcephaly brought things sharply back into focus. The condition meant that her brain had stopped growing during my pregnancy, rendering it small. Therefore, her developmental progress would depend on how much of her brain was functioning normally. Conversely, the degree of disability would depend on which areas of the brain were missing or damaged. At this stage no one could tell us what kind of outcome to expect with Cheryl. Consequently, the paediatrician's statement "She will never be normal" continued to echo in my mind like the throbbing of a bad headache.

I had delivered over forty babies, and given birth myself. It goes without saying that after a baby is born the mother's first question, once she has found out if it is a boy or girl, is: "Is he (or she) all right?" In the majority of cases the reply is also usually standard: "He (or she) is just perfect."

Those are the words every midwife wants to say, and every parent wants to hear. The stress of labour is always relieved with the announcement of that news – a perfect baby!

The world we live in today seems to be obsessed with perfection, or at least with its own notion of perfection. Many of us strive relentlessly to achieve academic success, which will in turn open up the perfect job opportunities, that will give us the financial capability to buy the big house filled with the perfect size-zero-wife and equally good-looking children. They, in turn, will strive relentlessly to achieve academic success, and on it goes. Meanwhile the rest of us look on and wish we could have a share in their seemingly perfect life, and spend our time trying to dip our toes into what we regard as perfection.

Undoubtedly, we live in the world of the designer label. What we wear is not nearly as important as who made it, and that others know who made it. This is so much the case that manufacturers often display their exclusive label on the *outside* of the garment. Why wear Ralph Lauren or Coco Chanel if no one else recognizes it? A lot of our teenagers would rather die than be seen in a pair of trainers manufactured by anyone other than those of the current trendsetting brands.

The goal of perfection invades many areas of our lives, not least what we wish for our children. We long for them to be perfect, to be healthy, to be successful, and to be liked by others. I was no different. Then when things don't turn out the way we expect, we reckon that it has to be someone's fault.

I wish I could say that I accepted Cheryl's condition without question, as so many other godly people accept dark and difficult circumstances, but I didn't. It is obvious to me now that I was just beginning to walk the long road of learning unquestioning faith. Then, at just twenty-three years old, I was tormented by questions with elusive answers.

The blame game is a dangerous one to play, and one that has no winners. What surprised me was the number of other players in my particular game. Players who had little previous involvement in my life, yet their cunning and often unwitting tactics added to the suffering of my soul. It amazed me the number of throwaway, hurtful and negative comments that seemed to cast a cloud which obscured the encouraging murmurings of those who cared deeply about my pain.

"Why did God give your Catherine a child like that?" my mother was asked. "When you think of all the evil women in the world today, and your Catherine's such a good girl." Mum warded off the comment with the disdain it deserved, but as I held my baby after hearing those words, I was astounded that someone would think of Cheryl as unworthy or simply not good enough for our family. She didn't fit the perfection mould.

A child's first birthday usually brings the next big influx of cards after the birth itself, but as news filtered through to friends across the world, we received little notes of encouragement and assurances of prayer long before that date came around. Having many missionary friends and others in Christian ministry at home has always been a source of delight. The ability to confide in like-minded people often helps to lighten the burdens you are unable to share with others. On one day a letter arrived with a foreign postmark that gave away the sender, and as I tore open the envelope I wondered who had told this ministry friend our news. The world is definitely a small place!

"Must be a sermon," I muttered, "there seems to be masses of paper here."

A small cotton handkerchief trimmed with orange embroidery floated to the floor as I unfolded the paper. Strange, I thought, as I settled myself down to read the epistle. It started with the usual greetings and I was touched by the sentiments, but it wasn't long before my jaw dropped and hot tears were stinging my face.

The author was setting himself up as a messenger from God to tell us that it was not His will for Cheryl to be this way, and therefore there must be some sin in our lives which had brought judgment on our family. We were to get on our knees and pray that God would reveal our sin, and after we repented, God would heal Cheryl. In the meantime, he had prayed over the enclosed handkerchief, and if we placed it on top of Cheryl, God would answer his prayer and start the healing process.

I was gobsmacked!

At one time this person had had an important spiritual influence on our lives, and although our contact had been only sporadic in the time leading up to the letter, I was shocked and further pained by his words. By the time Philip arrived home my hurt had turned to anger, and yet I was afraid that there might be some truth in what our friend had said.

"What if Cheryl is disabled because of something we have done?" I asked my surprised husband. "What if it's our fault?"

If we didn't put the handkerchief on Cheryl, could we be disobeying God?

Philip and I are so different. He is quiet and gentle, always prepared to look at what lies behind someone's actions, and not to jump quickly in judgment. At times it infuriates me, and at times I envy his measured and cautious approach. It usually means less repentance time for him, and much more for me!

He read the letter in silence, only the odd sigh hissing from his pursed lips. He was disappointed in what was written, even hurt. He let me release the torrent of my anger, then took me in his arms and let me cry. He's been very good at that over the years. Then, when the dust had settled, we discussed the comments made in this piece of unwelcome correspondence.

Scripture makes it clear that none of us is as we should be, because sin came into the world in the way described in Genesis chapter 3. It can also be proven medically that some sickness develops because of certain kinds of addictive or immoral living. But Jesus clearly tells his disciples in John chapter 9 that personal sickness is not necessarily a direct result of another's sin. The disciples asked Jesus if the man was born blind because of his parents' sin, and Jesus answered, "Neither this man nor his parents sinned, but this happened so that the work of God might be displayed in his life" (John 9:3 NIV). If any lesson can be drawn from this story, it is surely that sickness is more to do with the eternal plan of God than the current circumstances of an individual's life. This went some way to lowering the accusing finger that had tried to point blame in our direction.

"What should we do with this?" I asked my husband, as I stared at the crumpled handkerchief in my lap.

Philip reminded me that only once in Scripture was

there mention of people being healed after a handkerchief had been sent to them. On this occasion we did not feel that the sender warranted the same authority as that given in Acts 19:11–12: "Now God worked unusual miracles by the hands of Paul, so that even handkerchiefs or aprons were brought from his body to the sick, and the diseases left them…" These were unusual miracles, and while I do believe that God can still heal today, the accompanying misinterpretation of Scripture in our letter did nothing to give me any confidence in this limp piece of cotton.

Comments come and comments go, and I was much too busy to dwell on them openly, so they were often filed away in my subconscious to fade away or to be dealt with at a later date. How vulnerable is the hurting heart. My husband has a speech principle that is so wholesome: if it doesn't edify or exhort, then make sure you need to say it before you do. If only we were all so wise.

It is said that a first baby requires you to make lots of adjustments to your life. That's very true. Along with the normal newness of parenting came a whole different set of people and situations that we hadn't reckoned on.

Because of my job, hospitals held no major fears for me, but I was amazed at the number of appointments, clinics and professionals that were suddenly involved in our lives. On one day alone five different health professionals arrived at our home within the space of half an hour!

The Campbells really had entered the "disability lane" of a world that, until now, we knew existed but never imagined we would ever be part of. In this world we were to meet remarkable children, loving parents, dedicated staff and those whose job was to solve the strangest of problems with their technical skills. At times we grumbled when we thought the service was inadequate, but in truth, we don't know what we would have done without the various therapists who taught us how to work with Cheryl.

The therapy clinics quickly became part of our lives, and we are still in contact with some of the staff we met back then. When you work hands-on with a child over a long period of time it's hard not to make a personal connection. What was passed on at the clinics became the basis for Cheryl's daily routine of physiotherapy, handling and even feeding. Who would have thought that the way you eat can affect your ability to make sounds and even formulate speech; or that the way you are positioned for feeding can prevent you from getting pneumonia? For me, it was certainly a case of learning something new every day.

Medical outpatient clinics were a different kettle of fish. Generally speaking, very good relationships were formed over a number of years with the paediatricians who cared for Cheryl, but the forays to see consultants at predominantly adult hospitals were very stressful for both this mother and her child.

Cheryl's beautiful blue eyes looked normal, yet her visual response was slow. Only when a toy or shiny object was held close to her face did it stimulate any kind of a reaction. Sometimes we wondered if she did not reach for things because she found it difficult to do so, or because she could not see what we were waving in front of her. Wanting to give her every opportunity for progress, I was happy when the day came for the appointment at the eye department of a major hospital.

Philip dropped us at the front entrance and drove off to speak at an afternoon meeting, apologizing as he went for not being able to accompany us.

"No problem," I assured him, "I'm not expecting anything mind-blowing today. See you later."

Cheryl was snug and asleep when we reached what I can only describe as a chaotic and crowded waiting area. A considerable amount of time then passed before a harassed nurse called Cheryl's name. Explaining that her pupils would need to be dilated before the doctor saw her, she showed us into a square room with seats on three sides. The lighting was dimmed to reduce the discomfort of those who were waiting for their eye drops to work. The room was also jam-packed, and I squeezed into a seat between two people. Before I had time to lift Cheryl out of the buggy, the nurse hurriedly pulled down her eyelids and inserted drops into her eyes. Shocked, and with stinging eyes, Cheryl woke with a start, her crying the only noise to break the silence of this uncomfortable room. Glancing sideways I wondered if no one had ever heard a crying baby before, as people bristled and stiffened while I tried to calm my frightened daughter. It was not a child-friendly environment.

At the end of the room I noticed two curtained cubicles. Some patients disappeared behind the curtains, while others were whisked away in a different direction. Unsurprisingly, those of us who remained could hear every word that passed between doctor and patient behind the flimsy cotton walls – including diagnosis and personal details. So much for confidentiality, I thought.

The curtain was suddenly pulled back and Cheryl's name was called once more. With baby in one arm and pushing the buggy with the other, I moved forward with difficulty as the room continued to fill with an endless stream of patients. After a brief hello, the doctor quickly read the referral letter, and disappeared through an adjoining door. Some time passed, and he returned with a man who I can only assume was the consultant, as we were never introduced. The tell-tale accompanying entourage of medical students confirmed my suspicions.

How on earth are they all going to fit into this cubicle? was my silent question.

They weren't!

The curtain was left open so that all the students could see us, but it also left my private concerns and vulnerability visible to every person in the room. With nowhere else to look, and no escape, they were all drawn into a conversation they did not want to hear, no doubt longing for the proverbial big hole to swallow them up from the view of this distraught young mother.

"So you are concerned about her sight," the doctor remarked and, without waiting for a reply, he turned to the waiting students. "What do you notice about this child?"

There was no reply.

"Come on," he grunted, "it's very obvious."

Someone cleared their throat at the back of the group. "She has a small head," he said.

"Hold her up straight, Mum. What else do you notice about her small head?" he cajoled them.

By now I felt invisible, and my daughter a mere teaching aid in the hands of a learned but insensitive man.

"It's flat at the back," was another's reply.

"Exactly!"

Then without a moment's hesitation, or any sign of concern at what he was going to say in a public place about my child, the eye specialist launched into the next part of his lecture. He was talking to his students, and my presence was inconsequential. I was merely listening in as he explained how the vision centre in the brain had not developed, and therefore could not translate what was being sent to it from the eyes.

When he took his eyes off his adoring students to look at me, the only words he could manage were: "Your daughter has cortical blindness. There's nothing wrong with her eyes, it's just that she can't make sense of what is coming through them. No need to make another appointment, there is nothing we can do for her." With a flick of his hand he opened a path through the crowd for his retreat.

A subdued and somewhat embarrassed nurse helped me back to a seat, while the other shocked onlookers held their collective breath. As I struggled to put Cheryl's coat on, and hold myself together, the elderly lady beside me made a try at the only humanity I experienced that afternoon. With her hand on my knee she said, "I'm so sorry, Love, for your bad news." I don't know how I managed to get out of that department with dry eyes. Outside the rain mingled with my tears, and the passers-by didn't seem to notice the distraught mother as they rushed past to seek shelter.

Philip had seen us coming in the rear-view mirror, and jumped out of the car to rescue us from the downpour. His smile quickly disappeared as he realized that it was more than rain that was distressing me. I sat behind him in the car, holding Cheryl's hand as she sat in the car seat.

"She can't see," I blubbered. "Or rather, her brain can't make sense of what her eyes let in."

"But her eyes are OK?" Philip quizzed, unsure of what I was trying to say.

"Yes, but the doctor says that doesn't matter because her brain doesn't know what she's seeing."

I tried to explain further, and as I heard myself use the words "cortical blindness" it all became too much to take in.

"Doesn't she have enough to cope with, without being blind as well?"

Philip did not reply. But Heaven did.

It was as if God heard the anguish of my soul, and responded in a way I have only experienced a few times in my life. There was an almost physical presence in the car that stopped speech and thought and tears. In the briefest moment of time I felt the peace of God wash over me from head to foot, calming me intimately, and causing the weight in my chest to disappear. It felt like a bucket of cool water pouring over me on a hot day, relieving every sense. All that was left was an overwhelming feeling of the love of God, and a tangible experience of Philippians 4:7: "And the peace of God, which surpasses all understanding, will guard your hearts and minds through Christ Jesus."

By the time we reached home God's peace far outweighed any pain inflicted by an uncaring doctor or an unwanted diagnosis. Anyway, no one knew for sure precisely how much Cheryl could or could not see, so we went on treating her like a sighted child, stimulating her whenever, and however, possible.

The Campbells love birthdays, and as we were due to be away over Cheryl's first birthday, there simply had to be an extra celebration. Grannies, granddads, aunts, uncles, and a few visiting foreign friends all gathered for the big party in our rather small living room. Cheryl was in her element. She looked stunning in her elegant party dress, with accompanying lacy socks and enough shiny blonde hair now to cover her whole head.

Like any other little girl, she played the crowd that day, charming everyone in sight. You would have thought she knew she was the main attraction, smiling right on cue, and throwing her head back with a chuckle every time her knees were tickled. It was a genuinely wonderful day, and the many sad moments of the past year seemed to blow away with the flame of the solitary candle on her large birthday cake. As I tucked her up in her cot, after the visitors had gone, I felt the delight a firstborn gives. Others may have looked on her as different, but to me she was simply my Cheryl.

"It will be nice to get away," I said to myself, as I packed what seemed to be an inordinate amount of stuff for such a little person. I managed to convince myself that it would all be needed, so nothing was removed from the overfilled suitcase. We were off to help staff the TES family holiday centre, where over two hundred people would come on each of the three weeks for fun and Bible ministry. Philip was working for The Evangelization Society at the time, and most of the evangelists and their wives were roped into helping. Gifting didn't seem to matter as you could end up cleaning, helping in the kitchen, or on the games field. It certainly made me chuckle to see Philip in the role of sports officer!

Based at a private boarding school in the English countryside, the event was certainly not a holiday for the staff, but they do say that "a change is as good as a rest", and that's just what I needed. I could even make myself useful in the kitchen when I wasn't busy with Cheryl.

The journey from Northern Ireland was tedious, but as we turned into the long, tree-lined driveway I thought I'd never seen anything so beautiful in my life. The building that lay before us looked gracefully majestic. I could just imagine the rich and famous leaving their sons to study in such elegance. That is, until we saw the dorms, and then I thought we had been transferred to one of Her Majesty's prisons. They were unbelievably tatty, but at least we only had to sleep in them!

Work quickly got under way as the guests started to arrive. Families came from all over England, with a number of small church groups. One such group was from a Nigerian church based in London, and they had brought a number of babies and toddlers with them. There was a lovely enclosed garden which was used as a crèche while the morning Bible studies were in progress. As the weather was so beautiful, I decided to take Cheryl in her buggy to meet the other little ones.

On the path leading into the garden I was approached by a rather large lady in impressive Nigerian dress. I smiled as we met, only to hear her tutting in response. Before I could greet her she spoke, vigorously shaking her head as she did so.

"Shame, shame," she said. "Children like that shouldn't be born. 'Taint right. Better if she'd died at birth, don't you think?"

Dumbfounded, I stammered, "No, I *don't* think so."

My retreat was rapid, as I virtually ran through the maze of corridors to our awful little room.

"How could anyone look at you and think it would be better if you had never been born?" I said to Cheryl, glad that she could never be hurt by anyone's words because she was oblivious to their meaning.

In that instant I refused to believe she was some freak of nature, or even some kind of divine mistake.

"Surely they're wrong, Lord?" I questioned, as the old dorm bed creaked under my weight. "Show me they're wrong, Lord," I pleaded, as I lifted my Bible on to my knee.

It was one of those moments when I wished I knew my Bible better, so I'd know where to turn to get just the answer I needed. But in His wisdom, the Author of the book knew better than the reader what was needed just then.

I do not normally agree with the ad hoc approach of throwing your Bible open and hoping a verse jumps up and hits you between the eyes. Taking that as divine guidance is shaky to say the least. Far better to be regularly reading God's Word, and to hear Him speaking, than to use it as some kind of a quick fix to give you the answers you want to hear. Yet God, who recognizes not only our immediate needs, but our weakness in times of despair, occasionally displays His graciousness by speaking to us out of the unusual. Such was the case that day.

My Bible opened naturally in the Psalms, not surprising really, as David's poetry is easy to read when your concentration is poor, as mine had been in the previous months. I sighed, not really expecting to find what I was looking for there, and wondering if I should maybe turn to the book of Job. But I read on anyway, believing that God had heard my request for wisdom. These are the words He spoke to my heart from Psalm 139:13–16:

> *For you formed my inward parts;*
> *You covered me in my mother's womb.*
> *I will praise You, for I am fearfully and*
> *wonderfully made;*
> *Marvellous are Your works,*
> *And that my soul knows very well.*
> *My frame was not hidden from You,*
> *When I was made in secret,*
> *And skilfully wrought in the lowest parts of*
> *the earth.*
> *Your eyes saw my substance, being yet*
> *unformed.*
> *And in Your book they were all written,*
> *The days fashioned for me,*
> *When as yet there were none of them.*

"Listen to this, Cheryl," I exclaimed, making the poor child jump as I raised my voice in excitement. "You are no mistake, Sweetheart. God knew exactly what He was doing when He made you… it says so right here in Psalm 139. It says here that God formed you. He knew your little frame before I did, when it was just a bunch of cells – it wasn't hidden from Him. You were no surprise to Him. And, you know what, Cheryl?" I continued, gasping with delight. "God knows exactly how many days you will have here. You were meant to live, Sweetheart, and not to die. That lady was wrong, very wrong!"

I doubt she understood a word I was saying, but the excitement in her mummy's voice caused a big smile to cross her face. We danced around the room together; sure that God had not made some big faux pas with my daughter. I might not understand why He made her the way He did, but the knowledge of the sovereign hand of God from her very conception put paid to the nonsense that she was some unfortunate disaster.

Down through the years I have learned to see this world's view of perfection from a completely different perspective. Our *raison d'être* is far greater than health and wealth, happiness and beauty. Psalm 139 gave me the assurance that Cheryl was "designer made", and that stamped across her life were the words: "Made with love by God."

4

Changing Direction

The TES Holiday Centre was full of highs and lows for three long weeks.

I had experienced the euphoria that accompanied the knowledge that Cheryl was no mistake. Somehow God had a reason for her being as she was, yet alongside this knowledge was a reluctance to fully accept that she might never walk or talk. It is funny how the human psyche holds tenaciously on to the slimmest strands of hope. A doctor can take the time to explain all the possible scenarios of a particular condition, yet often the patient only remembers the one good thing he has said. It is an emotional protection mechanism, one I have often used myself.

Around the time of diagnosis, one of the paediatricians made a comment that I had turned on its head.

"If Cheryl doesn't sit up by the time she is a year old," he said, "then there will be a serious question mark over her physical development."

I had decided to miss the negative implications, and go straight for the positive.

"Then there is a chance that she might only be affected mentally," I had told myself. "She might even walk, if we can get her to sit up by her birthday."

So we worked with her day in, day out. Poor Cheryl was tormented. Every few weeks we would make the journey to see the physiotherapist, and I must have seemed like a dream mother to her, because I carried out the programme of physio exercises to the letter. Cheryl hated it, but I was convinced that all her discomfort would eventually be worth it all. Positioning, stretching and hanging precariously over large foam wedges only resulted in one thing – misery and tears.

Cheryl reached that magical birthday during our time at the Holiday Centre. The early family birthday celebration was boosted by a surprise party given by the staff, who had instantly fallen in love with this frail little girl. Cake, balloons, and a big teddy, accompanied by cuddles and singing, brought lots of smiles from Cheryl, which further excited her admirers. All the attention that was lavished on her helped take the focus away from me, and I was glad. It was hard to keep up the happy act that was hiding a very hurting heart.

Cheryl had reached the important milestone mentioned by the consultant months before. She was now one year old and she couldn't sit up by herself. In fact, she couldn't even hold her own head up without help. As my emotions did somersaults, I knew that could only mean one thing. There was now a question mark over her physical development. I couldn't ignore it any longer.

The next day I volunteered to chop the onions – enough onions to make chutney for 250 people. That's a lot of onions, but then I wouldn't need to explain my tears.

Onion chopping was done in a tiny little prep room cum store, off the main kitchen and discreetly hidden from the view of the other workers. It was the perfect place for my emotional dam to burst privately.

The only visitor was the kitchen porter. He was a humble, godly man who, although highly intelligent, worked his holidays as a general dogsbody to serve the staff, guests and ultimately the Lord.

"Can I help?" he asked.

I replied that I was managing OK, wishing he would just go away and leave me to my teary task.

"I'm not talking onions," he continued. "Can I help with whatever is upsetting you?"

He quietly leaned against the bench with his arms folded, awaiting my reply. Realizing that I had been rumbled, I surprised myself by telling far more than expected to someone I had met only two weeks earlier. Out it all came in a torrent of despair: the stuff about the birthday and how my hopes and dreams had been shattered. My disappointment, yes, even anger with God. My longing for Cheryl to be normal, and the deep annoyance I felt with myself for crying so much.

"I'm a Christian," I blurted out. "I shouldn't be falling apart like this!"

He was silent for a moment, while I blew my nose yet again, suddenly embarrassed at just how much I had revealed. Most men have difficulty knowing what to do with their own wives when they are emotional, never mind someone else's wife! His response was both gentle and strong.

"Do you believe that God made you?"

"Yes," I replied, rather bemused.

"Do you believe God made you with tears?"

"Of course," I retorted.

"Then if God made you with tears, it is perfectly all right to use them," he said, shrugging his shoulders. "No guilt required. The rest God will deal with in time, as long as you let Him."

His response was short, sweet and simple. No wagging finger of blame, no theological treatise on the sovereignty of God, just simple, loving advice from a compassionate heart. Afterwards he put his bony hand on my shoulder and prayed an equally simple prayer.

"Lord, heal Catherine's broken heart. Amen."

Peace returned, the onions were chopped, and the conversation between us was never mentioned again.

Dealing over the years with the constant ebb and flow of human emotions has been personally frustrating, and perhaps difficult for the onlooker to understand. One minute I experience the highs of God's peace and presence in my life, while at others I am wallowing in the depths of despair. There seems to be such inconsistency. However, I have come to realize that with the constantly changing circumstances surrounding Cheryl's condition, my reactions were merely only those of a mother.

We have been created human, with all that involves: joy and sorrow; peace and pain. What I find astounding is the patience of the Creator, as He consistently picks me up, dusts me down, and helps me on my way again. With the passage of time I notice less despair and more trust, as I very slowly learn the lessons He is trying to teach me. It is so good to be able to look at the great heroes of Scripture, like King David, and identify with their somewhat yo-yo existence. The fact that God did not give up on them fills me with hope.

Apart from the emotional and physical load Cheryl's condition placed on us, we were soon to realize that it wasn't only our dreams for our darling daughter that were broken. Since our late teens, both Philip and I had felt a real tug towards overseas missionary work. Philip studied missiology at Bible college while I completed my nursing training. We undertook both courses of study with the intention of being prepared to work in some country of God's choosing overseas. That dream was never to be realized. What missionary society would employ a couple with a disabled child? What parent would take their disabled child away from where she could get the best possible treatment?

We would have to learn to dream new dreams, and to accept a change in direction for our lives.

One month after that fateful first birthday Cheryl had her first surgical operation. The jerking, writhing movements of her muscles (athetosis) meant that one of her hips was not able to sit properly in its socket. If Cheryl was ever to stand, even with support, the surgery was necessary, and so we agreed to let it take place. On the morning of her first surgery, Cheryl sat on my knee smiling from ear to ear as her daddy captured the scene on film for posterity. All dressed up in a bright red woollen coat trimmed with white lace, she looked more like a child going to a party than to a hospital bed. For Cheryl everything was always a surprise. We could never prepare her for what might be difficult or excite her about what would be pleasant. At times it made me feel like a real heel.

This was one of those times.

When the fancy clothes came off and the flimsy theatre gown went on, I could feel my heart sink. Cheryl had no idea what was going to happen. As Philip and I walked beside the massive theatre trolley holding our precious child it was hard to think of what to say. She was still smiling when the staff whisked her away, and the swinging door pushed us back into the corridor.

"It feels as if we've betrayed her," Philip said as we walked hand in hand around the hospital site to help pass the time.

Yet that feeling was nothing compared to how we felt when we heard her screams as the trolley was pushed back into the ward. Too often we would have to make decisions that cut at our hearts, all because we tried to give our brave little girl the best possible chance at life. Thankfully she adapted fairly quickly to her new circumstances.

For the next three months Cheryl was in a huge plaster cast. It extended from her ankles to under her arms, with both legs spread out and bent up like a frog. What a head-turner she was, as we had to fill her pram with pillows and strap her on top, with both legs hanging out over the side! If it hadn't been so serious it would have been comical. What we did find comical, however, were the surprised looks we got as we ventured out for walks together. A few others were in danger of joining Cheryl in plaster casts as they engaged in rubbernecking to witness this unusual spectacle.

Those three months in plaster were followed by a further six months in similarly shaped splints, which proved extremely difficult for a child who could nothing for herself. Sleepless nights rolled into sleepless days, ad infinitum.

However, it was during this time that I became pregnant with our second child. Some time previously we had visited the geneticist to find out our chances of having a normal brother or sister for Cheryl. He was a lovely man, who gave us his undivided attention while we were with him. He even wrote upside down to enable you to read his notes as he was explaining the difficult subject of how genetic anomalies cause abnormal births.

He explained that there was no way to prove that Cheryl's microcephaly was definitely a genetic problem, as there was not a specific test available. It was his opinion, however, that it was a recessive gene disorder with a 1:5 chance at worst, or a 1:10 chance at best, of recurrence. A 1:10 risk did not sound too bad to me, and a healthy baby would make it all worthwhile.

After talking it over and praying, Philip and I decided that whatever the outcome, we would have the baby. There was no discussion, at any time, of a termination, whatever the test results would show. God's Word had already done its work in our hearts concerning the sanctity of human life, and interestingly enough I was not overly concerned during my pregnancy.

I was happy, puffy, excited and very tired throughout my second pregnancy. Cheryl didn't seem to notice my expanding waistline. Cuddles were not rationed, and that's all that mattered to her! Also, as I grew larger Granny and Granda took the extra strain, and they enjoyed every minute of it.

Extra visits to a special genetic obstetric clinic were slotted into my antenatal care, and they helped to encourage us that everything was going along just fine. The baby's head seemed to be growing at the expected rate, which was the only way microcephaly could be detected at this stage. Other tests for various deviations from normal all came up negative, causing a little whoop of glee after each hospital appointment. In spite of the tiredness, I really enjoyed being pregnant, and a December baby was going to add to the excitement I always have in the run-up to Christmas. Cheryl's splints came off in July, making things much easier for everyone, especially her.

Life was particularly lovely that autumn, and it was so nice for the whole family to share in being "normal", after supporting us through the heartache of the previous two years. We wanted them to have a healthy baby to enjoy as well, although their love, acceptance and devotion to Cheryl were always clear for the world to see. Only the visit in November of Philip's boss, the TES Director of Evangelism, stood between us and the big event, and we were even looking forward to that.

Bob's visit came around quickly. He was to stay with us for the first few days of the week, and then go on to the other TES evangelist for the rest of his time in Northern Ireland. Preparing for his visit was quite convenient, as it meant the house would have its final big clean before my due date, which was ten days away. Everything would then be ready.

Philip had just left for the airport when I noticed the discomfort in my back. I put it down to too much cleaning. Trying to ignore the ache, I promised myself a relaxing evening while they attended their first meeting, and set about making dinner.

By the time they arrived home I was wondering if I could be in early labour, as the backache was coming and going more like contractions than muscle strain. If I could just get them out again, put Cheryl to bed, and have a rest, I was sure the pain would settle. After all, I still had ten days to go, and Cheryl was ten days late – if that was anything to go by. The meal went off with pleasant conversation, and the men headed off, completely unaware of my little secret.

Cheryl was a gem that evening, and dozed on my knee in her soft cuddly pyjamas. Getting her to bed was a little more difficult than usual, with the pain in my back halting the procedure a time or two on the way upstairs. Afterwards, with a mug of tea resting on my bump, I decided it was time to have a little talk to my eagerly awaited son or daughter.

"It is time to settle down now," I explained, stroking the mountain I had been carrying around with me for nearly nine months. "Mummy has had a busy day, and you can't possibly come until Uncle Bob leaves in a few days."

Thankfully I never had a verbal response to any of my

mother/baby conversations, just the occasional kick or somersault! This time the response was a strong tightening of the tummy, accompanied by lower back pain that made me groan.

"Don't do this to me, baby. Not yet!"

Ten minutes later the performance was repeated, and ten minutes after that again. After a quick trip upstairs to check my prepared hospital bag and to leave Cheryl's clothes ready for the morning, I went into the kitchen to get supper organized.

I heard the men's voices, and quickly flicked on the kettle switch.

"Philip, can you come into the kitchen, please?" I requested.

After a peck on the cheek, and before he could launch into his report on a successful meeting I said, "I think I'm in labour."

His response was typical of a man who likes everything to be well organized, and on time: "Don't be silly, you're not due for ten days yet, and Bob is here. What can we do with him?"

Needless to say, rearrangements were made, and, five hours later, on 25 November 1981 at 3.30 in the morning, Master Paul Campbell weighed in at 8lb 14oz. He was big, with real boyish features and a head of dark hair. His wrinkled skin and loud cry made us laugh with joy.

He was so beautiful… and so perfect!

As I held him in my arms my hands glided over his head. Feeling the open soft spots in his skull just under the skin reassured me that all was well.

"Look at his lovely big head," were the first words I uttered to his dad as I nursed our new little son.

The staff exchanged a knowing glance, realizing the importance of such an unusual comment from this particular new mother. I thought nothing could compare with giving birth for the first time, but the sense of relief and delight this time round was overwhelming. God was allowing us the same opportunity given to the majority of parents, to have a healthy baby. We were in for a real treat, and one we did not take for granted.

Paul charmed everyone who saw him; even Cheryl smiled at the strange new noises in the house. It was not possible for Cheryl to be jealous of her new brother, she didn't know how, and grannies and grandas, aunties and uncles all managed to lavish their attention on both her and the new arrival at the same time. It was really like having two babies at once, only the younger was soon outstripping the older. Watching the speed of his development was amazing. Things that other parents took for granted filled us with wonder, from his ability to catch hold of his own toes and put them in his mouth,. to his dexterity in pinching Cheryl's soother out of her mouth and placing it in his own! Every day was a delight that helped us deal with what was going on in the life of his "big" sister.

Three months before Paul was born, Cheryl had started attending Segal House Nursery Unit. The unit is run by the charity organization Mencap, which provides help for children and adults with learning difficulties and their families. Segal House was unusual in that it provided multidisciplinary care for children from two years old with varying disabilities. Physiotherapy, speech therapy, occupational therapy, and the services of a social worker were all available to the children on site. That meant we could reduce the number of outpatient clinic appointments, while increasing the actual hands-on time with therapists.

Apart from therapists, the unit also had excellent classroom staff who cared for the children and helped to stimulate them through play. Added to all this, the family got a much-needed break for part of two or three days a week. Those days allowed me to have special time with Paul; time exclusively for him. Segal House provided a truly wonderful service, certainly appreciated by this family.

However, leaving Cheryl there for the first time was traumatic. We had come in contact with a few disabled children when waiting for appointments at clinics, but walking into the classroom at Segal House that day was something we were not prepared for. The room was beautifully bright, with nice smells and nursery music playing, but it was the children who took us aback. There were about ten severely disabled toddlers placed in different positions around the room. Some were lying on mats, others were being held, while a few sat in strange-looking chairs. I had never seen so many disabled children all together before, and for the first time I realized that we were not alone. In fact, many families out there faced the same challenges we faced from day to day. I was just unaware of the size of the problem until that moment.

We really did live in a different world now. Soon we would befriend people whose paths never would have crossed ours if it had not been for our precious children. At the parent support groups we discussed difficulties and shared solutions, or at least ideas. The issues discussed were diverse: from walking the benefits minefield to managing your child on public transport. There were also fun nights arranged, combining socializing with fundraising to enable the nursery to continue operating. Laughter was a release, while at other times we shared tears.

It was particularly sad to watch some marriages break up because the husband could not cope with the suffering of his child, or with the lack of attention he was receiving. We witnessed human nature at its best and occasionally at its worst. It taught me to pray for God's protection over our marriage, and to build a strong relationship with our young son. I vowed Paul would never become a second-class member of our family because of the time we had to spend with his sister.

The two and a half years Cheryl spent at Segal House Nursery were strangely settled. Apart from the development of epileptic seizures, her general health was pretty good. A daily routine of physiotherapy was worked into our lives, although it was disappointing to see how little progress she made. Cheryl was lots of work but no trouble, as she was such a sweet-natured child. My parents were a great help with the care of both children, while other family members threw in their lot with the babysitting.

Paul brought real happiness into our home, as he continued to delight us every waking moment. Cheryl did not always tolerate his constant kisses and hugs, even though he meant well. And we always had to keep an eye on his desire to share, especially the sweets he wanted her to taste! For Paul, Cheryl had always been there, and it was not until he was much older that he realized that his sister was quite different from those of his friends.

Cheryl's seizures brought a number of changes. It was difficult to know just how aware she was of what was happening, but it was disturbing for us to witness. We were also concerned to know why this was happening now, when she had been seizure-free for her first two years. Did it herald some kind of deterioration in her condition? We just did not know. The seizures required regular medication. This was the first of many drug interventions, and it brought with it the dilemma of treatment versus side effects. On top of all this, the kindly elderly paediatrician in whom we had so much confidence was about to retire, and he decided it would be best to pass Cheryl on to the newly appointed paediatric neurologist at the Royal Belfast Hospital for Sick Children.

The first clinic visit was a disaster as far as I was concerned. The new consultant might have been some kind of a medical genius, but that was not what mattered to me: what was important was how she treated my child as a person. She did not touch Cheryl, apart from doing "medical" things, and she never once spoke directly to her during our visit. She also changed Cheryl's anti-convulsant medication yet again. How I was going to work with this woman I didn't know, and I definitely didn't want to see her again. But we did have to go back – we had no choice – because Cheryl was always going to need a neurologist.

The second visit was better, with more interaction with Cheryl, and I could see that the doctor had a genuine concern for all of us. Over the next eighteen years this lady was to become a big part of our lives. We learned to trust each other with Cheryl's care, and a great respect developed between us. I can honestly say now that I would not have wanted anyone else in the world to have had the medical responsibility for my children. She was an amazing paediatrician; totally devoted to a group of children who are among the most vulnerable members of our society. I thank God for her, and I am so glad she was on our side!

Surprisingly enough, life became quite routine. Our family might have looked a bit different when we were seen in public – and we certainly didn't hide away – but this was *our* family, and perfectly normal to us. Being busy with two children meant I tended not to dwell on what I wished for, but got on with what I had. That is, until something or other came along to rock my boat.

For example, one Sunday morning I managed to get out to church while Philip was away preaching somewhere else. Both Paul and Cheryl were in the crèche, and I was settling down to enjoy the sermon. Our minister was a wonderful preacher, and I soaked up his message, especially as it was not possible for me to attend all the services any more. A good way into the sermon he made a statement that made my blood boil.

"We have no right to question the things that God brings into our lives," he said. "What He does, He always does for our good."

I have no idea what he said next, because I switched from listening to arguing with him in my head.

How dare you, I fumed silently, with fists clenched and lips pursed. What right have you to talk about questioning God? You with your perfect little family, your healthy, happy little boy and girl! What do you know about it?

To say I was angry is to understate the mood I was in. I have no idea where it all came from. I had left the house in good form, yet now I was inwardly displaying an anger I did not realize was there. How easy it is to file away in the subconscious all the feelings and hurts you decide not to deal with at the time. That day I learned how bitterness can weave its way into your being, and just how destructive it could be if you let it stay.

The sermon continued alongside the battle that was going on inside my heart. My parents were sitting next to me but totally unaware of my anguish. Suddenly I was brought back to the reality of the service by singing. It wasn't the congregation, as I first thought: it was the minister! I had obviously missed the bits where he showed his concern for those who were walking through difficulties; I was too busy waging my own private war with him. But God had broken through to deliver His promise to me yet again.

> *It will be worth it all when we see Jesus.*
> *Life's trials will seem so small when we see*
>   *Christ.*
> *One glimpse of His dear face all sorrow will*
>   *erase,*
> *So bravely run the race, 'til we see Christ.*

The words washed over my being; challenging, condemning, and healing. Then the tears came. I heard God say to my heart: "Catherine, I know it is hard. But *one* day it will be worth it all, I promise you. If only you could learn to trust Me. Be brave. Keep on running. I am right there with you."

And I was so ashamed – ashamed of my anger, my bitterness, and my blame. My poor mother sat with me while the rest of the congregation stood to sing the closing hymn. She thought I was crying because of the sermon, but that was only part of the reason for my tears. I was crying because I was sorry for my rage; sorry for allowing a root of bitterness to take hold of me. And I was crying because I didn't deserve God's patience. Yet once again He was displaying His love to me, and covering my life with His promised presence.

5

Joy – Given and Taken Away

Here we were again, at another outpatient clinic in another hospital, only this time I didn't know why we had been sent for.

Unusually, the hospital was only at the bottom of our street and it didn't take much effort to get there. "Community Paediatric Clinic" was printed at the top of the appointment letter, and an unknown doctor's name typed beside our allocated time slot. I was a little agitated at having to attend, as Cheryl was normally looked after at the "Children's" in Belfast. After polite introductions, I enquired why we had been sent for. It seemed that the local health trust was under some government obligation to see all special needs children in their area annually. The fact that Cheryl was already five years old and had never been sent for before was lost on them!

The clinic had no access to her present hospital records, so I had to respond to questions whose answers would simply be filed away and which would make no difference to her care. In my opinion it was a pointless exercise, but the doctor was pleasant, and we spent some time discussing microcephaly, each learning from the other.

During the conversation some mention was made of life expectancy, and it stopped me in my tracks. I had never thought about Cheryl's life being shortened. Trying to retain my composure, I questioned the doctor in a casual manner, as I didn't want him to know he was giving me information that I wasn't previously privy to.

"Is there a generally accepted life expectancy for microcephaly, then?" I queried.

"Children with Cheryl's level of disability rarely see their teens," he replied rather nonchalantly.

My heart was heavy as I walked the few hundred yards home. I guess that parents don't normally think of their child dying before them, even if that child has major problems. It's just not the thing to talk about. However that night as I lay in my husband's arms we talked for the first time of that awful prospect: the possibility that one day Cheryl might die. It brought the reality of her condition home to us and showed us the impact it would have on the whole family. As Cheryl was still only five years old, the teenage years seemed a long way off, so I determined that the information I had acquired at the clinic wasn't going to be something I would dwell on. I was convinced that our little girl had a lot of living still to do. Only occasionally did I allow what now lurked in the back of my mind to surface. More often than not it was when Cheryl was ill.

After that day, however, there were times I looked at Paul and dreaded the thought that he might be left an only child. He was such a sociable boy and now, as a toddler, he had great affection for his sister. He had talked from an early age, and would chatter away to her constantly. The fact that her only reply was a smile – and even they were coming less often now – didn't deter this faithful little sibling. He appeared to understand her limitations and on certain occasions, especially birthdays and Christmas, he got to open Cheryl's presents as well as his own. He even provided the breath to extinguish the candles on both their cakes at the appropriate times!

"What would you think of us having another baby?" I asked my surprised husband.

"Don't you have enough to do?" came his instant reply.

The conversation lasted on and off for a few days. We covered the subject from all angles. How would I manage another baby in my already busy schedule? Was the thought of another baby only because we didn't want Paul to be left alone? Was that a good enough reason? What if we had another child with microcephaly? The more we talked about it, the more excited I became at the prospect of another baby, and the less I entertained the notion that anything could possibly go wrong. I was sure Paul would love a sibling to giggle in corners with; someone who could share his secrets, and grow into the future with him.

No one could ever take Cheryl's place in any of our hearts, but the thought of losing her some day helped us decide to try for another baby.

Success was only a matter of months away.

The phone rang, and on answering it, I was surprised to hear a midwife introducing herself on the other end of the line.

"Mrs Campbell," she said, "there is a little concern over one of your blood results, and the doctor would like you to come back for another scan."

She waited for my response as I tried to steady myself. Thoughts were racing through my mind, not least the fact that microcephaly cannot be detected by blood test.

"Which blood tests?" I answered sharply.

She was reluctant to tell me, but I persevered until at last she said: "The alpha-fetoprotein is raised... but we don't want you to worry until we do further tests."

Stunned, I stood for a minute with my hand covering my mouth. "Spina bifida?" I whispered to myself. "It can't be! I can't possibly be having a baby with spina bifida – not when Cheryl has microcephaly!" I gathered myself together, trying to take a more measured approach. Putting on my midwifery thinking cap, I tried to work through the situation more rationally.

"Mrs Campbell, a positive alpha-fetoprotein test is *not* 100 per cent accurate for a diagnosis of spina bifida," she continued, probably now wishing she had not revealed so much information to me over the phone. I knew the midwife was correct, and so I agreed with her that the best thing to do was not to panic, but to wait for the hospital appointment in a few days' time.

The waiting was awful.

Only Philip and I knew what was going on, and if I hadn't been so pushy on the phone, neither of us would have had to suffer the accompanying anxiety. We decided not to send unnecessary shock waves into the family until we knew what was happening one way or another.

The day of the scan arrived at last.

The doctor took a long time moving the device slowly over my slippery tummy. All the while I was praying, my hands cold and clammy with nerves. Occasionally he uttered a few words, the most reassuring being: "The spine looks good to me, I don't know why the tests were reporting high alpha-fetoproteins." I breathed a huge sigh of relief. Yet he continued laboriously moving backwards and forwards with the scanning wand until he exclaimed, "I've found the problem!"

His loud voice made me jump.

"Problem? What problem?" I asked nervously. "I thought you said the spine was OK."

The tone of my comment brought him back to the reality of an anxious mother on the couch.

Turning the scan screen towards me, he pointed out a small black bubble. I shrugged my shoulders, indicating that I hadn't a clue what he was showing me.

"This pregnancy started out as a twin pregnancy," he explained, "but only an empty sac formed – there's no second baby. The sac is now being reabsorbed and throwing off proteins in your blood, hence the false test result. Good news all round: this baby is perfectly fine!"

The atmosphere in the room changed completely. Furrowed brows became laughter lines, and we set off home relieved and more excited than before, with his words ringing in my ears.

"This baby is perfectly fine!"

By the time my tummy was getting too large to pass off as overeating to an astute three-year-old, we told Paul the news that he was going to have a baby brother or sister. He danced around the living room, whooping with glee and causing Cheryl to wriggle with all the excitement. I'm glad we decided to hold off telling him until then, because the remaining weeks were filled with one question after another. They were all answered, I might say, with simplicity – we only gave him enough information to satisfy the curiosity of his young mind. A short stay in hospital for surgery to have grommets inserted in his ears dampened Paul's fervour, but it quickly returned.

As with my previous pregnancy, I attended for serial scans on a fortnightly basis, feeling a real sense of God's peace as the time passed. My final scan was carried out four weeks before my due date, and the obstetrician's enthusiasm towards my pregnancy continued unabated.

"Home in a boat, Mrs Campbell," he said as he wiped

the gel off my huge abdomen. "There's nothing wrong with this baby. This one's perfect!"

The remaining weeks passed with such excitement. A deep, overwhelming sense of joy came from all quarters as the word travelled far and near – Catherine's got the all clear. Wherever we went, cautious concern was replaced by expectant eagerness. Family and friends were able to relax with us. After all, there could be no more different pronouncements over two babies: "She will never be normal" and "This one's perfect!"

The obstetrician genuinely seemed to be as delighted as I was to find he was on duty when I was admitted to the labour ward. We had discovered that he wasn't just a good doctor, he was fun as well. We were sure of a few laughs to break the somewhat tense atmosphere that can surround the labour experience. The first laugh wasn't long in coming.

It was Sunday morning and Philip was due to preach at a church service in Belfast. He wondered if he would have time to go and preach, and still be back for his third child's entrance into the world. He shared his dilemma with the doctor, who gawped at him incredulously.

"Tell them to sing another hymn," he replied. "It'll probably do them more good than one of your sermons anyway. This baby will be here before you get a chance to step into the pulpit!"

As it turned out, he was exactly right.

Our beautiful little girl was born at 11.40 a.m. on Sunday 28 July 1985 – right in the middle of church service time. She was 1lb 7oz lighter than her brother, and even with her screwed-up face and wrinkled skin she was just a little dream. Another girl. I could hardly believe it! This time she was handed to Philip first, who was simply beside himself with delight. He kept kissing her sticky little forehead, while from the corner of the room came the retort, "I told you they should sing another hymn!"

All wrapped up in green surgical towels for warmth, our new little daughter looked so cosy as Philip put her into my arms. In the three years since Paul's birth I had forgotten how tiny babies could be. Her eyes were like saucers and her little nose looked squashed against her beautiful pink cheeks. Her hands felt satin soft as I put them to my lips to kiss them.

"Welcome, little one," was all I could say.

She took my breath away.

Soon after, Philip was packed off home to announce the good news, which all of Newtownabbey seemed to know before he reached there. It seems my sister had been standing outside our home church telling everyone about the baby as the service ended. I think invisible fireworks filled the sky, such was the delight expressed.

Back in the hospital I found myself alone for the first time with Joy.

"What else could we call her?" my husband had declared in the labour ward. "God has given us a perfect daughter!"

I couldn't have agreed more, so Joy she became, with Rebekah Joy Campbell eventually filling the requisite line on the birth certificate.

Cradling Joy in my arms I talked to her quietly.

"Let's have a closer look at you, little one," I said, bending down to kiss her. "I haven't seen your toes yet, you're so well wrapped up."

As I loosened the wrap my heart skipped a beat and I gave a quiet gasp. Her head looked much smaller than Paul's had, three years earlier. My hands gently but anxiously moved around her skull, feeling for the soft spots that should be quite large at this stage. The kite-shaped one at the front was there, but appeared small. Panic started to set in as I couldn't find the triangular one that should have been at the back of her head.

Then it hit me. She looked so like her sister – so like Cheryl!

I wrapped her up again, afraid to think; afraid to ask anyone to examine her.

"But the midwife did check her out," I reminded myself, "so she must be OK."

For the next few hours I played mental ping-pong, torturing myself one minute and reassuring myself the next. To and fro I went, convincing myself she was microcephalic, like her sister, then reminding myself of all the antenatal tests that had said she was perfect. The very doctor who was at her birth had said just three weeks earlier: "There's nothing wrong with this baby."

I was frantic.

"Please, God… please take away this awful fear, and give me Your peace," I pleaded. "Everyone at home will be so excited right now. I can't tell them how I feel." Then I convinced myself. "Of course she is like her sister. Lots of sisters look alike."

I was trying to replace panic with persuasion, reminding myself that Paul had been a sturdy big boy, while Joy was a fine little girl! Today was to be a day of celebration, and no silly thoughts from an overanxious mother were going to spoil it. So, strong-willed as I was, I determined not to say anything to anyone about my concerns until Philip and I were alone that night, during fathers' visiting time.

The baby and I were moved from the labour suite to the ward before visiting time. The place was frantic, and the excitement was palpable with grandparents and aunties cooing and fussing over the new addition. The fact that she was a girl seemed to add to their delight, and joining in with their happiness helped to settle my heart. No one else mentioned that she looked like Cheryl.

"New mothers are notoriously emotional," I thought. "Everything is fine. I am sure God wouldn't do this to us again."

After they left, I settled down to feed Joy. This time as I held her my feelings were only those of happiness, accompanied by the thrill I had denied myself only a few hours earlier.

"Your mummy is a silly woman," I said to Joy as I put her back in her little Perspex cot. Looking at her through the clear plastic I settled down in both heart and body for a very well-earned rest.

Philip arrived that evening, having had an afternoon sleep, looking more human and extremely chuffed to see his new daughter again. I let him tell me about all the phone calls he had made and the responses of delight they had brought. He explained how Paul was a bit miffed that he was going to have to wait until the next day to see his new sister, but calmed by the fact that he and Granny would come alone and not have to share the baby with anyone else. Cheryl had just smiled, probably more in response to being spoken to, rather than to the news she was given. It was only five days until her sixth birthday, and I wondered how she would respond to the feeling of a wriggly baby in her arms once again.

Philip looked the picture of contentment while cradling Joy in his arms on the armchair beside my bed. I felt guilty at disturbing his peace by mentioning my earlier fears. But we had worked at having a marriage that avoided secrets, and so I gently told him of my panic in the labour ward, and my concerns over the size of the baby's head. I could see both shock and disbelief cross his face at the same time. Initially he said nothing, while I felt a few little tears trickle down my cheeks. Wiping them off quickly, I watched Philip change the baby's position in his arms so that he could get a good look at her.

"Her head is smaller than Paul's," he agreed, "but she is smaller all over than Paul. I really don't think you should worry, Catherine, she's beautiful."

His comments made sense, and I promised I would ask the paediatrician about it when he visited the ward the next day.

It was nearly three o'clock and I was getting excited about introducing Paul to his new little sister. Suddenly he burst in through the door, pulling Granny behind him, and ran straight past me to the cot. With a flurry of activity he swung a tiny little pink bag in beside Joy.

"This is for you, Baby!" he exclaimed, stammering with excitement.

And in the same breath he turned to me and asked: "What do you call it?"

Explaining that the "it" was a "she", and that her name was Joy, I lifted my excited pre-schooler into my arms. He went on to tell me how he had taken money out of his piggy bank, and had picked her present all by himself.

"Do you like them?" he exclaimed to Joy, as he pulled a tiny pair of lacy pink and white socks out of the bag.

His loud voice made her wriggle, much to his delight.

"Let's try on her socks, Mummy," he said, at the same time pulling the blanket from around her.

Granny took control, lifting Paul up on the bed beside me, and then placing Joy carefully in his arms. He held her cautiously, almost afraid to move and biting his bottom lip in deep concentration. Granny tried on the socks, and we all laughed.

"They're too big, Mummy!" Paul shouted in disappointment.

"Just you wait, Paul," interrupted Granny, "I bet they'll fit her by next week!"

It was a lovely visit. As Paul turned to go he kissed Joy on the cheek.

"I love you, Sister," he said. "And I'm going to tell Cheryl all about you!"

Little did that baby know just how precious she would become to her big brother, and how protective his love for her would be.

The following day I returned from having lunch in the day room to meet the "baby doctor" coming out of my room.

"Just checked your baby," he said, "she's ready for home."

Blocking his exit, I surprised him by asking, "What do you think about the size of her head?"

He quickly looked at Joy's medical notes, trying to establish his authority in this uneasy situation. (The doctors who carried out the baby discharge examinations were usually the most junior on the paediatric rota, and they were not often asked difficult questions by mothers.)

"Her head?" he stammered. "What's wrong with her head?"

Guiding him back towards Joy's cot, I replied: "Don't you think it's a bit small in comparison with her length and weight?"

Glancing at the measurements he had taken, he became very defensive.

"It's on the lower limits of normal, but I'm not concerned," he blustered. "You nurses are always looking for problems. Why don't you just take this baby home and enjoy her?"

"But I already have one child at home with microcephaly. I don't think it is unreasonable to be concerned."

My last comment totally unnerved him. It was obvious he had not bothered to check whether there had been any antenatal concerns about this baby, making him totally unprepared for postnatal queries. He did not like my challenge, and continued commenting on fussy mothers who imagined problems as he made his withdrawal.

The fact that I had dared to question him was obviously reported to the midwife in charge, and when she appeared soon after in my room I felt like a naughty child. I needn't have, as she sat beside me and quietly asked what I was worried about. Unlike the young, threatened doctor, she listened carefully and took Joy out of my arms, running her hand over Joy's skull.

"Her head circumference is still within normal limits, Catherine," she said kindly. "If you are still worried in a few weeks' time take her to your own family doctor."

I felt as if I had done battle and couldn't wait to phone Philip to tell him that we were ready for home.

"Maybe the doctor was right," I said to myself. "Maybe I am imagining problems where there are none!"

Paul's excitement more than made up for Cheryl's lack of it as her sixth birthday dawned the day after Joy and I arrived home. Philip was delighted to have all his family back home, and he managed some party shopping while Granny and I handled the table preparations and the cooking. By the time our living room was filled with party-goers Cheryl was all dressed up in her lovely birthday frock, adorned by the big "I am six" badge picked out by her brother. She was in great form, and didn't seem at all bothered by the new noises in the house coming from her little sister.

As I looked around the room I couldn't help but feel so privileged that my children were born into an extended family who loved each one of them so very much. We were blessed indeed. Cheryl, who was small and slight for her age, cuddled up to her granda and I don't know which of them had the bigger smile. I was glad for the sake of her doting family that she smiled that day, as there were more and more days when she didn't, or perhaps couldn't. This would be a birthday we would remember for many happy reasons.

Joy, like her sister and brother before her, had an unsettled time with colic every evening. Apart from that she was a very good baby, feeding and sleeping well. It was during her waking moments that my concerns continued about her head size and poor muscle tone. She was still very young, but her floppiness was causing me anxiety. I took it upon myself to contact the physio from Segal House, with whom we had remained friendly after Cheryl had left the nursery to attend Hillcroft Special School.

At almost six weeks old, Joy was put through her developmental paces by our friend. Reflexes and responses were checked, and Joy was encouraged to perform like any other six-week-old baby. I could see as time went on that she wasn't doing very well.

"She's beautiful, Catherine," the physio said.

I could feel a "but" coming on, and I was right.

"But I think it might be a good idea to let Cheryl's paediatrician see her… just to check her out."

She went on to explain her concerns, promising that she would try to speak to the paediatrician before I phoned her secretary the next day.

Feeling like a lump of clay, I drove home, unable to muster emotions of any kind: surprised by how heavy empty actually feels. Suddenly I was unwilling to accept what had been *my* concerns about Joy in the first place. Philip, as was his usual practice, reacted more positively about the advice to get a paediatrician's opinion.

"Maybe this will settle your mind once and for all that everything is all right. I think it's a good idea," he said.

Three days later I was sitting in the waiting room of the busy paediatric neurology clinic with Joy on my knee. Never before had a hospital appointment come so quickly. Our friend, the physio, obviously had some clout with the paediatrician.

I knew the staff at this particular clinic well, yet none of the usual chat was forthcoming. It was almost as if the nurses were afraid to ask why our new baby had been added to the already full appointment list. They all busied themselves with other things, and I was glad. I didn't feel like chatting.

When Joy's name was called the usual parent/doctor introductions were not needed. This doctor knew me only too well, as Cheryl had a consultation with her on a regular basis. Leaning forward she gently stroked Joy's cheek, causing her to root and both of us to smile. The kindly touch broke the nervous atmosphere I had dragged in from the waiting room with me, and I was able to share my concerns with her.

Quickly and efficiently repeating the various tests carried out a few days earlier, the paediatrician handed Joy back for me to dress. After watching our little one fail these developmental checks yet again, I found it difficult to speak.

"We'll talk after you come back from X-ray," she said, aware of the silence that was creeping between us.

"I've asked one of the radiologists to do an ultrasound of the ventricles in Joy's brain, and he has kindly agreed to do it today."

I'm sure I looked surprised as she handed me the relevant request form. It usually took a few weeks to arrange such a test, so I meekly thanked her, and headed off to the X-ray department.

Some time later, ultrasound investigations complete, Joy and I sat in front of the doctor once more. A deep sense of foreboding was beginning to overwhelm me. How I wished Cheryl hadn't been sick that day. If she had been able to go to school then Philip would have been here with me. I suddenly felt very alone and vulnerable.

The doctor's first words said more than I wanted to hear.

"I'm sorry," she said.

How could two such small words reveal so much!

"The tests and ultrasound have shown that Joy's brain has stopped growing," she continued, even though I knew exactly what she was going to say. I wanted her to stop right there and for me to be able to run away from those damning words. But she kept on talking... just like the doctor had done six years earlier.

"She has microcephaly – just like her sister. I am so sorry."

Joy started to cry, and I realized it wasn't only my breath I was holding tightly. Loosening my grip slightly on my baby allowed a restrained sob to escape from my lips. Before I could reach for my handbag, the doctor landed a pile of hankies on my knee. The tears came, but no words. I couldn't speak. I just wanted to go home. I *needed* to go home.

With a foggy haze covering my mind and heart, my only words uttered were directed at the windscreen of my car as I tried to escape. But I knew there could be no escape.

"It's not fair, Lord! It's just not fair!"

I remember leaving the hospital, and I remember arriving at my front door, but I don't remember how I got there. There was obviously a myriad of guardian angels protecting us that afternoon as I drove through Belfast's busy Friday-afternoon traffic. Thankfully, Paul was at his friend's house when his distraught mother arrived home that afternoon, and Cheryl's high temperature kept her asleep.

Philip took Joy out of my arms, as I stumbled through an account of the events of the day, weeping. I felt so cruel telling my lovely husband that his darling little Joy was going to end up like his beloved Cheryl – never able to walk, or talk; never able to sing or play; never able to plant kisses on our cheeks or speak our names. The pain was unbearable, and unremitting tears flowed at that dark, dark moment.

A few hours later, after composing ourselves somewhat, we took the girls with us to break the awful news to both sets of parents. Paul stayed at his friend's house for tea, and we decided not to tell him for a while yet that his precious baby sister was disabled. We wanted him to enjoy her as a baby first and foremost. Having the girls with us gave the grandparents something to do with their arms while they listened to news that broke their hearts once again. They grieved not only for their grandchildren, but also for their own children who were hurting so much.

The news spread like wildfire.

Soon we were surrounded by an outpouring of love and attention from friends and neighbours as well as family. Apart from the odd unkind comment like "It's a pity they didn't content themselves with the two children they already had," we were overwhelmed by kindness. So much kindness, in fact, I was afraid that Paul would know that something was up, what with lots of visitors and frequent whispering. He was almost four years old, and I thought it would be too hard for him to understand; he just loved being with his little sister and I didn't want that to change.

However, situations often have a way of working themselves out in a way that we could never plan.

A few days later Paul was on the floor drawing a picture, when, without even lifting his head he said matter-of-factly: "Mummy. Is Joy handicapped – like Cheryl?"

I nearly fell off the sofa. Panic set in. I wasn't ready for this and I started to stammer.

"Would you still love her if she was handicapped?" I asked foolishly, not knowing what to say.

Paul tutted in response, still concentrating on his picture. "'Course I would… silly Mummy!"

Oh, how badly I had underestimated the loyalty of our affectionate young son. Calling him to me, I sat him on my knee, realizing that it was time for the truth.

"Yes," I replied, squeezing him close. "Joy is disabled, but we will keep on loving her just as much as we love Cheryl."

"I'll give her my picture, Mummy," he replied, and jumped off my knee, unperturbed, to finish his masterpiece.

My rainbow seemed to be dissipating.

God's promise to me six years earlier was that He would be with me through every storm and cloud. Now, however, I couldn't sense His presence at all. In its place was enormous disappointment and sadness. For six years I had experienced His help. For six years I had rested in the knowledge that God knew what He was doing. I had learned so much over that time from His Word, and could say that I had been to places with God that I had never dreamed possible. Spiritually I was a different person from the one I had been before Cheryl was born. Yet for the first time since then I felt unsure of His love. My heart was empty, and my mind was exhausted from trying to work out what good could possibly come out of all this.

"Have I not learned enough, Lord?" was my frequent cry of despair.

Day seemed to follow day with no break in the darkness. I functioned at the level of necessity, while trying to avoid being in public if I could help it. Tears let me down too easily, and I didn't want to disappoint others with my hidden feelings of disappointment with God.

Having watched Cheryl's condition deteriorate over the years, I knew exactly what to expect for Joy. That was the heartbreaking part. I knew *exactly* how badly disabled she would be. With Cheryl we hadn't known what was around the corner, and that protected us in some way. But with Joy we already knew the road she was about to travel and it was hard to look at this little baby, knowing what lay ahead.

It just didn't seem fair.

In time I would understand that God didn't promise to be fair as we understand it – He promised to be right. Determining fairness requires the ability to see both sides of the situation, and with eternal things that won't be possible for us until we reach Heaven. What is required for now is trust.

One thing I did learn over those years was not to neglect the Bible, because this is how God communicates with us. Closing the Bible is like refusing to allow God to speak. With all that I knew about Joy I desperately needed to hear Him speak. Each day I seemed to have a dark cloud hovering over my head, and I was finding it hard to concentrate. While feeling so emotionally low I found it helpful to use a book of devotional readings. It only required reading one small verse for each day along with the accompanying "thought" given by the author.

A mere five weeks after the news of Joy's diagnosis these are the words I read from 1 Peter 1:6b–8a: "You have been grieved by various trials, that the genuineness of your faith, being much more precious than gold that perishes, though it is tested by fire, may be found to praise, honour, and glory at the revelation of Jesus Christ, whom having not seen you love."

That day's "thought" described the conversation between a customer and the owner of a china shop. The customer wanted to know why one set of china had a design on it that stood out more distinctly than all the rest. The explanation given was that it had more work done on it – it had been put through the fire twice in order that the design would shine like gold!

I gasped as I read the words, "through the fire twice". I was touched that the black ink on the page I was reading contained further evidence of God's understanding of this particular mother's heart. God was speaking directly into my life once more. And in the darkness of my sadness I could see something glimmer: the faint colours of a rainbow – the return of God's promised presence.

"Catherine, can you trust Me with the things you don't understand?" He whispered to my heart. "Will you allow Me to work on you, in order that My glory might be seen?"

I suddenly realized that I was experiencing only the earthly part of a much bigger story, and that helped me to respond positively for the first time in weeks.

"Yes, Lord. But only if You don't leave me to walk alone!"

The colour of the rainbow brightened in my heart, as I remembered that this promise had already been given.

6

Unwitting Angels

L ife was very busy with three children, two of whom required everything to be done for them. In reality it was more than the usual "everything" that very young children require. Physiotherapy, along with various other therapies, had to be added to the mix. Then I had to incorporate hospital visits, clinic appointments plus other sundries, such as fittings for wheelchairs and buggies. Oh, and not forgetting all the extra professionals who visited our home. Remember also the fact that there was no such thing as a full night's sleep – ever! – and I think you might just begin to understand what I mean by busy.

While all this was going on, Paul was enjoying reaching the "big boy" stage and heading off to school every day. Usually about thirty minutes later the yellow school bus rolled down the street to pick up Cheryl. I doubt whether there were any mornings when I got off that particular bus after securing Cheryl into her seat without a smile on my face. Special needs children are invariably welcoming and good natured. So we were always greeted with hellos from those who could speak, and happy noises from those who couldn't. Sometimes we had to examine new toys, or hear the latest news from the passengers, especially after Christmas or birthdays. It's a wonder that the bus ever arrived at school on time! Still, we learned so much from these wonderful children about the simple things of life. Their ability to be happy and content with what we would regard as very little always astounded me.

School for Cheryl was very different from what Paul was experiencing. For her it was not about books and blackboards, but rather a home from home where she received care and stimulation. Large colourful paintings, usually displaying seasonal scenes, covered the walls of her classroom. Sensory equipment and toys stood waiting to be brought to life by eight little pairs of hands each morning. Beautiful, relaxing smells greeted those who entered, while cots and soft mats offered the opportunity for the frail pupils to rest.

Success in education for Cheryl and her classmates was measured by the appropriate response to touch, sound, or visual objects in whatever programme was being used. The staff had amazing patience and even love for the children. Cheryl's teacher reported on the class activities in her home/school diary so that we knew what had taken place each day. Any seizures, how well she ate, and any other delights or disasters were recorded to fill the gap in our knowledge that Cheryl was unable to fill by herself. The diary meant that we could chat to her about school, and the staff could talk to her about home with the information we exchanged. In addition, the open visiting policy in Cheryl's room was of great help to those parents who felt uneasy about leaving their profoundly disabled child in someone else's care. All of this combined to make Hillcroft School a very special place.

While Cheryl and Paul were at school I enjoyed special time with Joy, particularly during those early baby days. It is important that each child is treated as an individual and we tried, where possible, to interact personally with each one every day. Whether it was cuddles and stories with Cheryl, or building castles with Paul, each had that unique time built into their lives.

I had heard it said that "normal" siblings can often feel neglected in a family that has a child with special needs. I find that hard to understand, as Paul was such a blessing in our lives, and watching him grow helped us enjoy the true delights childhood brings to a family. Through him we were introduced to the fun element of parenting, experiencing the excitement of watching his many skills develop. Paul's use of language started very early – in fact, we often laugh about the fact that he could talk in sentences before he could walk! You can imagine the thrill it was to hear those first words, as well as the ongoing delight of being able to engage in conversation with at least one of our children.

From Paul's earliest years he and his dad had a day or afternoon out together every week – just the two of them. Mummy wasn't even told where they were going; it was their secret until they returned. Sometimes it was something as simple as a trip to the park, or the swimming pool; occasionally a ride on a train, or a visit to the cinema. They even went on "Captain Planet" patrol, collecting discarded cans and exchanging them for pocket money. Mind you, their excursions usually included an ice-cream or a drink and a doughnut afterwards! Those special outings continued for years and I don't know who enjoyed their time together more, father or son. Time with our children is always the best investment we can make in their lives, and giving time to Paul was no chore.

Life continued at a normal-for-us pace after Joy's diagnosis. Cheryl had remained small for her age, but I became concerned with the increasing episodes of vomiting that seemed to blight most of her days. She was losing weight and feeding her was taking longer, with less enjoyment on her part and concerned frustration on mine. And so, for the first time since her hip surgery, Cheryl was admitted to hospital for investigation of the problem.

It was a Saturday morning. Philip was away in Scotland preaching, and Granda was holding the fort at home with Joy and Paul while Granny and I visited Cheryl. While we were chatting with the staff nurse, explaining that I would return after breast-feeding Joy, I noticed something alarming out of the corner of my eye. Cheryl, who previously had been restful, suddenly lurched forward and then fell back into the pillow. Her breathing was noisy and fast, and her pale cheeks had turned an alarming grey colour. Something was badly wrong.

The staff nurse turned on her heel to get a doctor, while I ran to Cheryl. She was clearly unconscious and unable to respond to her mummy's pleading voice. My organized nurse's mindset helped to keep me outwardly calm, while inside I was panicking, praying frantically as I turned my very sick daughter on to her side. At least the outward veneer meant that I was allowed to stay with Cheryl while the medical team swung into action. In a short time oxygen was administered, monitors were in place, and an IV cannula was put into her arm ready for whatever drugs they felt Cheryl needed. Unfortunately, they didn't know what the trouble was – so a more senior doctor was sent for.

When she arrived I was asked to wait outside while Cheryl was examined. I never liked being out of the loop as no one knew Cheryl, or her problems, better than I did. However it did give me time to speak with my mum, who was great at taking control when things went wrong.

We were just in the process of agreeing to Joy's first-ever bottle feed when the doctor interrupted our conversion.

"I think you need to get your husband here as quickly as possible," she said. I tried to explain that he was in Scotland, but she interjected: "It doesn't matter where he is, you need to get him home now. Cheryl is very sick."

I was stunned into silence, and could feel my mother gently rubbing my back, just like she did when I was little. The doctor had my undivided attention as she continued.

"I think Cheryl is in 'status'."

She explained that a continuous epileptic seizure was in progress, and that it was preventing Cheryl from regaining consciousness.

"We have no idea if or when it will stop – it's continuing in spite of the drugs we've given to her."

I didn't want to ask her the question that was searing my heart like a red-hot poker. I didn't want to speak the words that shouted in my head.

"Is Cheryl going to die?"

Mum broke the silence, her words staccato as she thought on her feet.

"I'll go home and get in touch with Philip, and bottle-feed Joy. You are needed here with Cheryl. Soon people will be praying, Love. Try not to worry."

She knew her last words were virtually impossible, but I bit my bottom lip and trembled as my mother took me in her arms, and tried to hold back my tears to avoid upsetting her further. Releasing me from her embrace she bravely went in behind the bed screens to kiss her darling granddaughter goodbye, unsure whether she would see her alive again. Then, with the sound of Mum's footsteps disappearing up the corridor, I was finally allowed to sit with Cheryl. Even my finally released tears dripping on her face didn't make her stir.

"Surely she can't be so sick," I thought; her colour had slightly improved now that she was receiving oxygen.

"Your daddy will be in such a panic, Cheryl," I whispered, as my thoughts were momentarily diverted to Philip receiving such news and trying to arrange to travel home quickly.

"O God," I prayed, "please let him get home in time."

It was only after the staff had finished working with Cheryl that I was suddenly stopped in my tracks with a disturbing thought. It was Saturday afternoon, and on the phone the previous evening Philip had told me that the evangelism team were hoping to see one of the big Scottish football league matches, while they were over there. This was before the invention of mobile phones, so I was in a quandary, wondering how on earth Mum would be able to get in touch with him. But God knew that Cheryl and I needed Philip, and He was working out His own plan.

When I phoned Mum a short time later, she told me that she had only just got through the front door at home when the phone rang. It was Philip, ringing to see how everyone was before he went to the football match! Instead of a relaxing afternoon off, the poor guy was given the news that he had to come home straight away. It was to become one of the worst days in his life. Frantically, Philip tried to arrange a flight home, but to no avail. There were simply no seats available from Edinburgh or Glasgow – not even when he explained his dilemma. In the end a friend had to drive him all the way from Edinburgh to Stranraer to catch a ferry. That man was the first of our ministering angels that day.

Every minute that passed seemed like an hour, and with each minute there was no change in Cheryl's condition. All we could do was wait. Inactive waiting causes the mind to wander, and rarely does it wander into good territory. The futile "what ifs" came with forceful frequency, destroying peace and heightening a sense of hopeless anxiety. What if… Cheryl didn't recover? What if… she died before her daddy got home? What if… she does recover and is left worse than before? What if? What if? On and on it went, until my "what ifs" became completely ridiculous. Those two little words are undoubtedly the devil's torment of the soul. Resting my elbows on the bed, I covered my head with my hands in despair and didn't hear someone approach.

I jumped when I felt a hand gently touch my shoulder, and looking up from my despair I saw my minister. The poor man arrived at my darkest point, as I was drowning in "what ifs". Undoubtedly God had sent him, because I needed his quiet, gentle counsel at that time.

A family man himself, and clearly disturbed at the sight before him, he sat at the other side of Cheryl's cot, holding her tiny hand tenderly. After a while of chatting over the happenings of the morning, he sensed that there was more going on in my heart than Cheryl's medical emergency.

"So what is really worrying you, Catherine?"

Some might have thought it was a strange question to ask under the circumstances, but he was spiritually astute.

"Will Cheryl go to Heaven if she dies?" I blurted out.

Stammering, I poured out the hidden questionings that were tormenting me at that time. Explaining that Cheryl didn't have the capacity to understand about sin and salvation, I told him I was afraid.

"What will happen to her?" I repeated.

He barely flinched, but in his soft Welsh accent he gently rebuked me.

"Ah, Catherine," his voice lilted. "Do you not know your God? Of course she will be in Heaven, for Jesus Himself said: 'Blessed are the pure in heart, for they shall see God.'"

He then reached into his pocket and pulled out his Bible. For the next few minutes we looked together at the story of the death of King David's baby son, and he read David's words to me from 2 Samuel 12:23: "I shall go to him, but he shall not return to me." Looking at me firmly he spoke words that I never forgot.

"If Cheryl dies she will go to Heaven, because Jesus said the pure in heart will see God – and one day you will go to her, just as we have been reading."

The issue was settled once and for all in my heart. Even on that darkest of days God was willing to minister peace through His servant. Deep down I had always known this to be true, but I didn't know where to look for the biblical evidence that brought the *absolute* assurance that I needed.

The time passed slowly as my minister sat with me – mostly in comfortable silence. I was so glad that I didn't have to be alone at that time, in spite of the fact that the staff were constantly checking on Cheryl's condition. And I knew it would take time for other family members to reach me.

Suddenly I heard a baby cry in the distance.

"I know that cry," I said, as my best friend turned into the ward carrying an extremely fretful Joy.

"She doesn't like the bottle. She has decided only her mummy will do!" my friend exclaimed as I gave her a hug.

The minister retreated while my friend deposited Joy into my arms. The sound of my voice calmed her for a few minutes as we quickly exchanged information on what was happening at home and with Cheryl. Soon Joy was happily feeding with only the shaking of her remaining sobs interrupting the scene. As she fed I learned that Philip was on his way to Stranraer to catch the ferry, and that Granny was contacting everyone for prayer.

As Joy's ministering angel was putting on her coat to whisk her back home to Granny, she informed me that another friend was organizing a rota.

"What kind of a rota?" I quizzed.

"We are all going to take it in turns to bring Joy in for her feeds every four hours, until this emergency is over. We don't want the wee mite miserable now, do we?"

I cried again, this time humbled by the love and support given to me by such a great group of friends, most of whom were busy with babies and families of their own to look after.

Thereafter for the next few days, every four hours, Joy was brought to the ward for a feed and a cuddle, and then taken away again, happy and content. I did feel sorry for the people who were doing the late and early morning feeds, though! During the night Granny persevered with the bottle, whether Joy liked it or not. And the staff, who affectionately named the service "meals on wheels", also had an early introduction to another child they would get to know well in the future.

Cheryl remained unconscious until late that night, opening her eyes literally ten minutes before her daddy arrived off the ferry from Scotland. She woke up as suddenly as she had fallen unconscious twelve hours earlier: her breathing settled almost immediately, and all her vital signs returned to normal. The doctor was still checking her out when a very stressed and exhausted Philip entered the ward. I rushed to meet him while the doctor brought him up to date.

"The worst seems to be over, but she's not out of the woods yet." Directing her comments to Philip she went on to say, "I'm sorry we had you rushing all over the country, but we couldn't predict which way this was going to turn out."

He was only half listening as he leaned over the cot to kiss his darling daughter.

"Oh, Cheryl, you have no idea how glad I am to see you, Sweetheart." Relief at seeing her alive erased the stress lines that had been imprinted on his face during the long journey home.

Soon Cheryl was in a settled sleep, and Philip and I talked quietly into the night, filling in the missing details of the day for each other. Over the next couple of days Cheryl had a few frightening relapses, but once she was stable enough we were able to take her home. Even those shaky few days could not prepare us for the many times we would find ourselves in the same position, with Cheryl fighting for her life. And on each occasion we would learn more about true Christian love and friendship, as family and friends pulled out all the stops to help us over and over again.

The Bible has plenty to say about angels.

Way back in the book of Genesis, Abraham had a visit from three men. They turned out to be angels sent by God with a special message for Abraham and Sarah. That message was to change their lives in the giving of a son in their old age, heralding the birth of a nation that would one day produce the Messiah. In 1 Kings 19 Elijah was in a state of despair when he was visited by an angel, who ministered to him in the most practical of ways, by providing food for him and encouraging him to rest. That particular angel was none other than the Angel of the Lord, the pre-incarnate Christ; further evidence of the compassionate heart of God towards His children.

Then in Hebrews 13:2 the writer reminds us that like

Abraham, we too may encounter *"angels unawares"*. In other words, we may not recognize them as such, but they are in fact messengers from God sent to meet our needs. God has myriad different ways of showing us that He loves us and that He hears our cries for help. I believe one of those ways is by using family and friends as his angels.

Just as with Abraham and Sarah, God often uses these angels to bring us a message from Himself; usually one of love, comfort and concern. At other times these angels are like the One who visited Elijah, bringing practical help and meeting a present need. Whatever the task, be it only once or over an extended period of time, these people become God's angels – just like the man who drove Philip to the ferry, and the friends who operated Joy's "meals on wheels" service.

Throughout the many crises over many years I have been the happy beneficiary of countless ministering angels. Sometimes a bunch of flowers lay on the doorstep awaiting my return from a long bedside vigil at hospital, simply saying: "Praying for you". Meals were made; ironing lovingly smoothed; children babysat; school runs undertaken; carpets vacuumed; shopping provided and even dirty clothes taken away to be washed. Often I was overwhelmed by the selfless actions of those who loved our family, who went far beyond the bounds of friendship, demonstrating the sacrificial love of Christ in tangible ways.

You may be thinking I have quite a group of friends, and you would be right. But I have also learned how important it is to accept help when it's offered! Many of us turn away ministering angels because we don't want it to appear that we can't manage by ourselves. Pride then blocks the answers to our prayers, and then blames God for the burden we think we must carry alone. We not only stop God blessing our lives, we hinder God's blessing on the lives of those who are responding to His request to act as His messenger.

God not only used our friends in the very helpful, practical tasks that made our life so much easier, He used them for our spiritual well-being too.

In times of crisis I frequently felt physically exhausted and emotionally low. Often this was brought about purely by the enormity of the situations we had to face. On occasion, concentrating was so difficult that I could read my Bible only in short snippets, while praying was sometimes beyond my emotional capability. There were days when I just didn't know what to pray for any more. Was it right to constantly ask God to bring Cheryl out of some crisis, just to face another one a short time later? What should I pray for concerning Joy? At times it was all too much.

It was at these times that some of my "ministering angels" became my intercessors as well.

"Let me do the praying," a friend said tenderly one night when I simply didn't know what to pray for any more. "Concentrate your energy on being her mummy, and let me bring Cheryl to God."

And she wasn't the only one. People all over the UK and friends throughout the world wrapped us in their prayers during the times when we felt too weary to pray for ourselves. We didn't only know it as a fact; we actually experienced it as we frequently sensed the presence of God creep into Cheryl's ward on occasions when all other hope was gone.

"Someone's praying," I would whisper to her in the darkness of many a night as situations changed and hope returned.

It reminded me of the story of the Old Testament

prophet Elijah, when he was faced with the distraught widow whose son had just died.

"Give me your son," said the prophet to the weeping mother.

Then taking the boy in his arms he laid him out before the Lord, and God miraculously answered his prayer by restoring the boy to life. There are no greater words that we can say to any distraught parent, whatever the cause of their distress, than these words: "Give me your child. Let me take him to the Lord for you."

This weary mother was only too glad at times to give her daughters to others to take to the Lord on her behalf.

Friendship is undoubtedly one of life's greatest gifts, and I know for sure that some of my friends are God's angels. How I thank God for them.

7

Riding the Roller Coaster

The surgical ward was unfamiliar territory to us all. Cheryl was normally nursed in the medical ward, where we knew the staff well and they knew us. In these new surroundings I felt insecure, unsure of how the nursing staff would cope with a child with such diverse needs as Cheryl. Most of their little patients were "normal" children in hospital for various surgical procedures. The surgical consultant was the only one known to us, as we had met him at the outpatient clinic.

As a nurse I understood both the benefits and the drawbacks of treating patients in specific specialist units. It meant that the best possible care could be given for a particular condition, with the staff very knowledgeable in one area of expertise. Problems arose when you had a patient with complex, multiple needs, the majority of which you had no expertise in: a patient like Cheryl. There was also an increased risk of mistakes occurring, especially if you didn't know the child, and that child had no way of communicating with you. For our peace of mind the only solution was to make sure that a family member was with Cheryl at all times during her stay.

Cheryl's vomiting was seen as the cause of her earlier medical emergency. Her anti-epilepsy drugs had to be maintained at a certain level in order to work effectively, but Cheryl was unable to keep them down, which meant that the drug level dropped, causing life-threatening, continuous seizures. Drastic measures were now required. A large hiatus hernia had been discovered during the investigations, and this appeared to be the root of the problem. Surgical intervention was arranged; hence our admission to this unfamiliar ward.

Cheryl duly went off to theatre, and after what to us was an agonizingly long wait, she returned to the ward. The staff did their best in caring for her, and were not unfriendly towards us as a family, but the whole atmosphere made for an unsettling time. The ward was frenetically busy – and so noisy! Not only was it not conducive to recovery, but the frequent, sudden noises startled Cheryl, making her jump. The jumping exacerbated the pain in her large tummy wound as she had no way of protecting herself from it. She couldn't hold her tummy when she went to cough, or tell you when she felt nauseated. The whole experience made her miserable. It was hard to watch. As soon as I could persuade the doctors, we took her home. At least there she was able to rest quietly, and we were hopeful that the surgery would improve her general health significantly.

Once recovered from the actual surgery, Cheryl improved for a short time, but not as much as we had hoped. Feeding was at times a long-drawn-out process, often taking up to an hour and a half. The surgery had made swallowing more difficult; this particular "cure" had only succeeded in swapping one set of problems for another. At least it stopped the vomiting... for a while.

The writhing muscle disorder (athetosis) that accompanied Cheryl's microcephaly was not only responsible for many of her disabilities, it was also the eventual undoing of her surgical procedures. The hip that had been repaired when she was thirteen months old was now permanently dislocated, pulled out of position by those dysfunctional muscles. Mercifully it was not painful, as it was not weight-bearing. Unfortunately, the dislocation caused her spine to twist, which led to severe chest deformity, which in turn led to breathing problems. Then, about a year after her surgery and before her eighth birthday, the work carried out on her stomach started to loosen.

There were times when we felt guilty at putting Cheryl through surgery, yet because we wanted to make her life as comfortable as possible we took some risks. At the time we made the decisions we had no idea that the underlying problem that necessitated both surgeries would also lead to the undoing of the work.

I guess we would also have felt guilty if we hadn't allowed the operations to go ahead, but it did help us to be more cautious when surgery was mentioned down the line for Joy.

So we entered a phase when Cheryl was not only a disabled child, but often a very ill child as well.

We tried to keep her days as normal as possible, sending her to school when she was well enough, and involving her in most of our family activities. There were always plenty of grandparents and aunties around to give both her and Joy cuddles at the various birthday "dos" and Christmas celebrations. We took delight in the things many other families took for granted. It was always worth the effort, even when it came to transporting all the special equipment necessary for both of the girls.

Special trips to see friends, usually in the summer, became real treats. Close friends of ours lived on the Ards

Peninsula in County Down, and we had many happy days with them while both sets of children were small. Paul particularly enjoyed having friends to play with, and usually prepared for our trips to the country several days in advance. He was always a performer, and while his sisters enjoyed his piano playing and storytelling, they couldn't enter into his desire to put on "shows". So you can imagine his delight when suddenly he had *five* other budding performers to work with, and a big house and garden in which to stage the show! It was great for us parents too, as we were left in peace to enjoy each other's company while rehearsals were in progress.

Tickets were designed and coloured by the youngest members of the Cloughey troupe. Props salvaged from garage and shed were painted by those thought more responsible in the group, and costumes gathered from wardrobes all over the house. (Our hosts were extremely co-operative with the visiting producer.)

Finally, when the little ones were about to wilt, the show was introduced with great excitement and fanfare.

"Ladies and gentlemen!" the noise bellowed through cardboard loud-hailers. "Come and see the greatest show on earth!"

The children's giggles were stifled by a stern look from Paul, who at seven was the eldest, and took it all very seriously. Once our tickets had been collected, the four of us, along with Cheryl and Joy, were shown to our seats and the show began. We might have been a small audience, but we were very appreciative, clapping and cheering in all the right places. The "Cloughey Circus" had acrobatic acts, singers, and even magic tricks performed by a magician in a black cape!

You can guess that it didn't take much rocking to get the children to sleep that night. It was only one of many such fun-filled days that we enjoyed with different friends and their families. From Waterford to Cloughey to Ballynahinch, special days with special friends made our good times even better. Their children always treated the girls with tenderness and understanding. Kisses, cuddles and face-stroking were enjoyed as much in the giving as in the receiving.

One friend's little boy always insisted on holding Cheryl's feeding bowl while I fed her, even though a table was available. He was very patient, as it could take forty-five minutes and more to empty the bowl. But it was his way of helping Cheryl, even to the point of missing the odd game outside with his brother and Paul.

This loving action was to be repeated often in the future for Joy by a very devoted cousin, who always wanted to be by her side when our families were together. The heart of a child can teach us so much.

Many were the precious memories for us to hide away in our hearts – times that make us smile, even today.

The day both Cheryl and Joy were admitted to hospital *together* felt really strange. Cheryl was seven years old, while Joy was one. In fact neither of them was ill, but both of them were to have brain scans carried out, and so the doctor decided to "kill two birds with the same stone", metaphorically speaking. It was only an overnight stay, and the staff suggested that Philip and I take advantage of the situation and have a night out together, with the promise that they would look after the girls well. Since we're into metaphors, we didn't "look a gift horse in the mouth", and enjoyed a nice evening out without the pressure of rushing home.

While we were blessed with selfless babysitters, their number decreased as Cheryl became weaker. So the lot often fell on my parents, without whom it would have been virtually impossible for the two of us to be out of the house at the same time. They carried out tasks that many grandparents would have cringed at – and without a word of complaint. Our love and admiration for them knows no bounds.

We were unsure of what to expect when we attended Outpatients for the scan results. The consultant had both scans clipped to the X-ray box when we entered the room.

"It's remarkable," she said, nodding her head, while we took our seats. "It's quite remarkable," she repeated.

I became impatient: "What's remarkable?" I questioned.

"You would think both of these scans were of the same brain," she replied, "except that the name is different on each of the films. This one is Cheryl's, and this one is Joy's," she said as she pointed.

We listened carefully as she tried to explain the complicated films. Even as a nurse I recognized that I was out of my depth with this, so I was glad of her detailed explanation.

Although six years separated the girls in age, the scans showed that their abnormal brains were identical – with one exception.

"See here," she pointed as she continued to speak.

This time we could make out what she was pointing to. Little white patches were visible on Cheryl's scan; whereas Joy's had none. The doctor went on to say that she couldn't be absolutely sure of the cause of these strange patches, but they did indicate little areas of damage to the brain tissue.

"Perhaps her seizures have caused the damage," she

theorized, "or it may be an indication of straightforward degeneration of the brain."

We didn't like the sound of either possibility, but were left with the impression that Northern Ireland's only paediatric neurologist felt that Cheryl's condition was deteriorating. In fact it was her impression that Cheryl wouldn't have too many birthdays left. While my heart sank, I held on to the fact that no one really knew how much time Cheryl had left – except the One who made her. And so I put on my stoical mask and we took both girls home, where we could get on with the business of being a family.

However, the thought crossed my mind that maybe it was about time we starting talking to Paul about Heaven, and what that would mean for Cheryl. I suppose denial caused me not to include Joy in the equation at that time.

"Will Cheryl be able to eat potato crisps when she goes to Heaven?" seemed like a perfectly logical question for a five year old to ask! Paul often lamented over the fact that Cheryl was unable to enjoy such delights, and if Heaven meant Cheryl could eat all the goodies that she missed here, then maybe Heaven would be OK.

While wanting to get across the reality of Heaven as an actual place, where pain and suffering would not be present, it was rather difficult to get the theology simple enough for a youngster to understand. We wanted Paul to know that one day his sister would get a new body, and one that would work perfectly. So with the help of his children's Bible, and other books especially written for children, we brought up the subject of dying every now and then over the next few years.

Death is still one of the great taboos for discussing with our children, yet I have found that if approached properly, preparation can be a great help to a child when someone they love dies. Many of their questions will have already been answered to some extent, and that in itself helps to reduce the element of fear.

Fear of the unknown can conjure up all kinds of imaginings. As his parents, Philip and I wanted Paul to learn about death in a way that was neither morbid nor would make him afraid. Even more, we wanted him to know about Heaven – after all, it must surely be the greatest promise ever given by God to those who are His children! While not wanting to dwell unreasonably on the topic, we found that it was Paul who inquired at the most unusual times about what was going to happen to Cheryl.

One day my hands were full with pushing our specially adapted twin buggy, and Paul was riding circles around us on his bicycle on the way to the local shops. The girls nearly landed under his wheels when he stopped abruptly right across our path.

"Paul!" I shouted in rebuke, while pulling the large buggy to a stop.

Before I had a chance to continue he looked at me intently and said, "Mummy, will Cheryl be able to ride a bike when she comes back from Heaven?"

The question floored me, and the public situation was not a suitable place for an answer that might upset him. Riding a bicycle in Heaven was one thing, but riding a bicycle *when she comes back* from Heaven was quite another.

"Let's keep that question for Daddy when we get home," I quickly replied, explaining that he needed to concentrate when he was cycling, or he would cause an accident. With his attention diverted for a while, I groaned.

"He must think that Heaven is a bit like going on holiday – when you've had your fun, you come back home again."

Later we gently told Paul that when you go to Heaven it's for good. You don't come back, but your family can go to you when they die. His face became contorted in thought, and then he made an announcement before returning to play.

"Don't think I like that. I want Cheryl to come back when she gets her new body and then she can play with me!"

It was just as matter-of-fact as that. He wasn't upset; he had just decided for now that he would rather she came back and that was that. Reasoning would have served no purpose at the time, and so we let that part of his childish rationale remain. It was enough for now.

Joy was very like Cheryl in her disabilities, but that was all. Their personalities were completely different. Cheryl had a quiet, gentle nature. She was a patient child, and by the time she was eight years old her hair was still blonde and wavy, setting off beautiful blue eyes.

Joy, on the other hand, at two years old was wriggly, giggly and full of personality. She responded to tickling, and could occasionally be calmed and frequently excited by music, much to her brother's delight. Needless to say, every toy in our home had to make a noise – even the storybooks had noise-making attachments. Her hair had lost its blonde streaks and was now a mousey-dirty-fair colour, like her brother's, and as straight as a poker. Her hazel eyes often glinted with a mischievous look.

As Cheryl became weaker her days were becoming even quieter, while Joy's days were filling up with Nursery School, appointments and therapists. Joy only crossed town to Segal House in Belfast for two terms, as a new nursery class had opened at the school in Newtownabbey where Cheryl was a pupil. It was strange, yet comforting, to see them head off in the morning together. And for the first time in two years I had a few hours each day to myself. It was wonderful.

By this stage Cheryl was spending most of her days asleep: nature's way of conserving her limited energy for the important tasks. Feeding continued to take hours every day, as her swallowing problems increased, along with the recurring stomach symptoms. There was no suggestion of further surgery, and so a variety of medicines was tried to alleviate the discomfort. Unfortunately some medications can interact badly with others, and on one occasion Cheryl was rendered unconscious by that very problem. It was a major learning curve for all the doctors concerned, and resulted in the doctor in overall charge of her care insisting that she be made aware of *any* change in Cheryl's medication. When you are under the care of four specialist consultants, each trying their best to alleviate the problem within their area of expertise, accidental errors may occur.

We had no intention of making it into a big issue as there was no doubt that our daughter was receiving the best care possible from a group of wonderful paediatricians. In any case, once the alterations in the regime were made, we got back a slightly more awake Cheryl!

Caring for Cheryl at home as much as possible was very important to me, and because of my nursing skills I was able to achieve this most of the time. The school physio was also amazing, and when Cheryl had one of her frequent chest infections she came to treat her at home. When Cheryl was in hospital it caused the added pressure of my being away from Joy, and rearranging Paul's schedule too. Thankfully, because Philip worked from home, he and my parents were able to manage, while I spent my days with Cheryl (and sometimes the nights too, if necessary).

And so we entered what I called the "roller-coaster" season of our lives with Cheryl. It's undoubtedly one of the hardest parts of caring for a life-limited child. You are brought to the edge of your physical and emotional strength so many times that it becomes exhausting. For weeks you could be making a slow ascent, when everything seems to be improving, and you dare to get excited that maybe the doctor was wrong – maybe she will see her next birthday after all. Then suddenly you plummet down to the depths of despair, feeling that you will never recover from being this far down. And then you turn a corner, levelling out once more, and watch the child you love start to climb again. All the while knowing that another drop is just ahead – except that you don't know where or when.

Thankfully, Cheryl didn't seem to be in too much pain. Her main problem was that her deformed rib cage made it easy for chest infections to settle, while also making chest physiotherapy less effective. We had battled through predictions of gloom for three birthdays and three Christmas seasons.

"She won't see her birthday," we would be told, only to watch Paul blow out the candles for his frail sister one more time.

"She won't make it to Christmas," the doctor's words echoed faintly while we were surrounded by all our lovely family members from far and near, celebrating yet another advent season.

"Thank you, Lord, for giving us another year," I would whisper as I tucked her tiny frame up for yet another night on this long journey of suffering.

In spite of a magnetic longing to keep Cheryl with us, it broke our hearts to watch as life began to lose its grip on her. Pathetically thin, she slept for most of the time, yet seemed to rally after every illness. The carriage of our roller coaster seemed to struggle to recover more after each drop: our excited responses were now muted as all the straight track appeared to have been removed. Yet she was such a brave little traveller on this harrowing ride, and we loved her more than words could ever convey.

So time and again when I lifted her in my arms I would talk to her about Heaven, just as I had with baby Barbara ten years previously. Because we are spiritual beings, I believe that God's Holy Spirit can reach into the places we know so little about. And so I would pray that He would give Cheryl His peace – as only He could. When things were difficult, and she struggled for breath, I would sing to her of the promise that God had given to me when I fought against His plan for my life and that of my first-born.

"It will be worth it all, Cheryl... when we see Jesus."

Later many people, including nursing staff, remarked on their sense that Cheryl had such a peace about her – it was almost like an aura. On those occasions I knew that God had answered my prayer.

I woke with a start and looked at the clock. It was nearly eight o'clock. We had overslept! This was unheard of, as we rarely got more than three hours' continuous sleep any night, and the girls (especially Joy) were always awake by six o'clock in the morning. Philip jumped out of bed to waken Paul for school, while I rushed into the girls' room.

Joy was awake and had wriggled her way under her duvet. If she had been able to speak I'm sure she would have cried, "Quickly, Mummy, rescue me! I'm roasting under here!" A big smile crossed her face as I lifted her out of the bed and handed her to her bedraggled daddy as he came into the room.

"Well, who's been a good girl, then," he said, "letting Mummy and Daddy have a lie in?"

She continued to charm us as I looked at Cheryl's sleeping form in the bed opposite to Joy's.

"Come on, sleepyhead," I said, "you'll never be ready in time for the bus this morning."

Bending over to pull back the duvet cover, I realized something was wrong. Cheryl's breathing was laboured, and her forehead was very hot as I planted my good-morning kiss on it.

"Oh, no, Cheryl," I groaned. "You're not coming down with this flu, are you, sweetheart?"

In December 1989 the news was full of reports of flu sweeping the country. It was the biggest epidemic in many years and it was severely stretching the health services. As I lifted Cheryl out of bed, she didn't even twitch. Concern enveloped me as she hung limply in my arms while I carried her downstairs.

Philip had already started feeding Joy her Readybrek when I entered the living room. His look darkened as he watched me prop Cheryl up on the settee.

"What's wrong, Catherine?" he asked anxiously.

"I think she might have this flu," I replied. "She just won't waken up."

I always tried to play down a crisis with Philip and Paul until we were sure that one really existed. So I encouraged Philip to continue getting Joy ready for school, while gee-ing Paul up at the same time. After quickly sponging Cheryl and giving her some rectal medication to help bring her temperature down, I made the decision to ring the doctor. Miraculously for early morning, I got through at the first attempt, and as soon as I reported that Cheryl could not be roused, one of the GPs came immediately. As the health centre was only a short distance away, she arrived within minutes.

"There's not much air moving in her lungs, Catherine," she said after sounding her chest. "I think we need to get her into hospital."

Perhaps it was denial of the seriousness of her condition, or genuinely because I thought she would be better away from hospital during a flu epidemic, but I persuaded the doctor to let her stay at home until I could get in touch with the school physio. I felt sure that if her temperature came down, and she had some chest physiotherapy, she would waken up and be able to take the antibiotics the doctor had left for her. The doctor was not convinced, but gave me a little leeway.

"You have one hour," she said as she left. "If Cheryl is no better by then, she has to be admitted."

It was still before nine o'clock; as Philip was leaving to take Paul to school, I was trying the physio's phone number at Hillcroft. About seven minutes later she was in our living room with her hands on Cheryl's chest.

"Please, Catherine," she pleaded, "take her to hospital. She is very sick!"

Everything in me wanted to shout. I wanted to keep her with me. I didn't want her to go into hospital. I guess what I was saying was that I didn't want her to die. It was only a few weeks to Christmas, and I was convinced that we could beat the doctor's predictions one more time.

However, I knew I had to give in, and within a few minutes the family doctor was contacted once again, and we were in the physio's car on our way to the ward. Philip remained behind to see Joy on to the school bus, with the promise that he would follow on behind.

The carriage of our roller coaster was hurtling downwards at breakneck speed and I could do nothing to stop it.

8

A Christmas Missed

I don't know what the doctor had said to alert the ward staff, but they were ready and waiting for us when we arrived at the hospital. A cot had been made ready in the four-bedded unit used for the very sick children. I had only ever walked past this room before, saying a prayer as I did so in recognition of the heartbreak represented there. It was what I considered a "quiet room", as children cared for in it were usually too sick even to cry. Now my own sweet child was to occupy a place in its confines.

My heart was racing as I laid Cheryl down on the cool white sheets, but I was soon to discover it was not racing nearly as fast as hers.

The ward doctor quickly examined our little girl, who was now fighting for her life. Her breathing was so laboured and rapid I could hardly keep up with the count as the nurse tried to measure it. An intravenous line was expertly slipped into place, and the first dose of antibiotics slowly passed into her bloodstream while the nurse taped the cannula in place. Monitors bleeped their sorry tale of a heart under stress, while an oxygen tent now kept me apart from my tiny ten-year-old.

Before Philip arrived the portable X-ray machine had trundled in and back out again, holding the secret of what was going on inside our precious girl. By the time her daddy had hurried to be with us, Cheryl looked really ill.

"If only I'd kept her at home," I thought, as I saw his worried face coming towards me. "She always looks worse when they attach all this equipment."

My deep longing to try to protect our darling child from this moment surfaced in irrational denial. My attempts at comforting Philip failed miserably as I tried to convince him that everything was going to be OK.

"She's come through it before, she'll do it again," I whispered, unable to muster the confidence that usually bolstered the people I loved.

Philip sat quietly as I rattled on. He was finding the hospitalizations harder and harder to bear, as with each one Cheryl grew weaker. Now, lying in the bed, she looked so weary, and I knew that Philip's fear reflected my own.

What if Cheryl was tired of fighting?

The doctor broke into our thoughts when he appeared, X-ray in hand. Pulling up a chair beside us, he sighed.

"I'm afraid things don't look too good. Cheryl has patches of pneumonia in both lungs."

We made no reply, waiting for the inevitable "but" that would assure us that it was only a matter of time before things improved. This time the "but" didn't come. Instead he explained that the consultant had been informed of Cheryl's admission, and that she would come and speak to us after her clinic.

After he left, someone brought us a cup of tea.

I'm always suspicious of cups of tea given without being requested. They smack of bad news, and are usually ordered by someone who knows more about what's going on than you do. At least drinking it gave us something to do, as we each escaped back into our own anxious thoughts. Soon Philip was on his way home to let the family know what was going on, and to make contact with the many prayer groups who had prayed for Cheryl in the past.

Alone once more, I created a little space in the walls of the oxygen tent to slip my hand through. As I held Cheryl's tiny hand the tears welled up and silently coursed down my cheeks. She had been here so many times before and had always proved the doctors wrong by getting better. It was less than three weeks to Christmas. She couldn't die now! I wouldn't let her. My heart felt like a stone in my chest, as I closed my eyes and prayed for the first time since waking that morning.

"Don't let her die, God, please!" was all I could say.

By lunchtime, the consultant had been to see Cheryl.

"I don't know if she'll see Christmas," was all I remember her saying.

"But you said that *last* year," I reminded her, "and she made it then."

The consultant screwed up her face with that "I-won't-be-wrong-this–time" look as she ordered the oxygen tent to be taken down and replaced with a more traditional mask. At least I was now able to stroke Cheryl's face again. I longed to hold her, but was discouraged from doing so, as my arms around her chest might restrict her breathing. Soon Philip returned, and during the day family members came back and forth, helping to fill the long day as we sat and waited. But still Cheryl didn't wake up.

As the week passed I made the odd foray home for a shower and to visit the children, while Philip stayed with Cheryl. Occasionally I brought Paul back with me when Philip and I changed shifts. We had discovered on a previous occasion that Paul fretted far more if he didn't get to see Cheryl than he did when we tried to protect him by keeping him away. His visits usually consisted of a hello to his sister, and then a trip to the ward play area which, in his words, was "cool".

Although it was a very difficult week, we experienced what I called the cotton-wool-treatment. We were so aware of other people praying for us and for Cheryl, that we felt "wrapped up" in the warm love and kind consideration of others. Sometimes I felt that Philip's was the harder job. He had to field numerous phone calls when he returned from the hospital late at night – exhausting but necessary to fuel specific praying.

Yet in spite of all those prayers Cheryl still didn't waken up.

When the consultant visited on Friday there was still no change, except for the fact that now she also had the flu, as did poor little Joy, who had been moved to Granny's for extra care.

Saturday morning came with a sense of excitement in the ward. Many of the children were out of their beds very early, and giggles were coming from the play area. I walked up the ward to see what was going on.

"We just can't settle them down," the nurse explained as I approached, "so we've decided to let them make paper decorations."

Strips of coloured sticky paper filled the table, as happy little hands excitedly made them into links for the growing paper chain.

"The Christmas decorations go up today," she continued, in a voice raised above the happy chatter.

Christmas! I had almost forgotten about the approaching holiday season as I had spent all week in a secluded four-bedded ward.

Returning to Cheryl's bedside, I was about to tell her about all the activity in the play area when I noticed something that made me gasp.

Cheryl's eyes were open – she was awake!

I turned on my heel and ran for the nurse. Neither of us could believe it. Cheryl moved her head, and her arms wriggled by her side. I thought I was going to explode with joy. She'd done it. She'd done it again! Already, in my mind, I was planning the great escape. A couple of days and she would be eating again, and then we'd get her home. This was definitely one Christmas we weren't going to miss!

I rushed out to the phone to tell Philip the great news. Soon the word would get around that Cheryl was getting better. She'd really done it! I could hardly contain myself. What a morning. Even the little paper-chain manufacturers couldn't beat the excitement felt further down the ward.

After a little while I was able to wash and dress Cheryl, and although she had a sleep afterwards, it was a normal restful sleep. Even the children on the ward entered into our delight. They all seemed to recognize the significance in the waking-up of the little girl who had been asleep all week, and they were excited too. In fact, shortly after nine o'clock, a small group of children were allowed to come into the unit where Cheryl and the other very sick children were being nursed.

They had glittery decorations in their hands. Tinsel was tied to Cheryl's cot, and a big picture of Santa was stuck to the wall close by.

"That's for Cheryl to see, now that she's awake," the little boy said proudly.

"I'm sure she'll love it," I replied, not wanting to spoil his fun by telling him that Cheryl couldn't see.

I waited impatiently for the first visitors of the day to arrive. I longed for someone to share in my excitement. Now I was able to hold Cheryl for the first time in a week, and she seemed to cope with it very well. Her bony little frame felt wonderful in my arms, and when Granny sang to her later that afternoon she even let out a gentle responsive "Ahh." Smiles replaced frowns, and praise replaced prayer. Everyone who saw her that day was rejoicing.

Later that evening Philip suggested that I go home for a sleep in my own bed, while he stayed on in the ward with Cheryl.

"I'll come home later if she stays settled, and you can come back in if you want. Go on," he coaxed, "Paul will be so glad to see you for a wee while."

The thought was enticing, and so I went home, secure in the thought that I would see Cheryl later.

Paul was in a lively mood when I picked him up from Granny's to take him home. Joy would stay there so that I could get a good rest, and I was looking forward to having all my family together again soon. The two of us sat and talked over his week, and he told me all about school, and his friends, and how glad he was that Cheryl was getting better. At eight years old he loved to please and was still very affectionate with his kisses and hugs. After talking for a while he jumped down off the sofa, and disappeared. I had no idea what he was doing, but when he reappeared I was bowled over by his thoughtfulness. He approached me with a tea towel hung neatly over one arm, like a waiter, and handed me a handwritten menu as he spoke.

"Madam, can I get you something to drink?" he said, putting on a posh accent.

On the menu card were written the words: "TEA OR ORANGE JUICE. TOAST OR BISCUIT."

"What's all this?" I asked him.

"I know you're tired, Mummy, and I just want to give you a treat," he replied, and then reverted to his actor's voice. "So, Madam, what would you like?"

As I didn't fancy explaining a scalding to a casualty doctor, I played it safe, choosing the orange juice and biscuit, which came served on a lovely tray complete with napkin. The thought, however, was much more appreciated than the food.

Once Paul was safely tucked into bed, I propped myself against the pillows and lifted my book of daily readings that I hadn't touched all week. Contentedly I started to read. I had barely finished the first paragraph when the words I was reading caused me to gasp.

> *Be strong, my soul!*
> *Thy loved ones go*
> *Within the veil, God's thine, e'en so;*
> *Be strong.*

> *Be strong, my soul!*
> *Death looms in view.*
> *Lo, here thy God! He'll bear thee through;*
> *Be strong.*

Anon

I closed the book and threw it down.

"No! It can't be true!" I exclaimed. "Cheryl is getting better. That word isn't for me. It can't be!"

The ringing of the phone interrupted the frightening thought that I had just read. It was my friend and we spent the next few minutes talking about how Cheryl had made a fool of the doctors once again. Soon, sleep overtook me.

I was exhausted, yet years of "listening" while sleeping in case the girls wakened meant that I woke up in response to the slightest sound. Philip was home, and I sat up as I heard his footsteps on the stairs. He looked tired as he related how the evening had gone. We decided to set the alarm clock for 2 a.m. in order that I could go back to the ward. Philip was not as happy with Cheryl's condition as he had been earlier, but he felt that I should get a bit more sleep before returning. The staff nurse in charge was one we particularly respected, and she had promised to phone us if there was any deterioration before then.

I decided not to share with him what I had read earlier. It was surely just coincidence. So I settled down to sleep again for another few hours, while Philip went downstairs to get a cup of tea.

Warm breath on my face started to waken me. In the distance I could hear my name being called ever so gently through my sleep.

"Catherine, Catherine."

In my semi-wakened state I realized it was Philip's voice I was hearing, and I suddenly opened my eyes to see him kneeling beside the bed. I knew what he was going to tell me as soon as I saw his tear-stained face. A look of deep pain stared back at me.

"She's gone!" he wept. "Our little girl is gone!"

9

The Final Farewell

How Paul stayed asleep through the noise of that night, I will never know.

My mind was in a whirl, with both grief and questions battling for prime position.

"She can't be dead!" I yelled at my upset husband. "They would never tell you over the phone that she was dead – you're wrong!"

His attempts at comfort were met with agonizing distress, as my world fell apart around me.

"How could we have left her to die alone?" I wept. "Why did the nurse not phone us in time? We should have been with her!"

My voice lost its strength as I stopped fighting the man I loved so much, and fell into his arms.

"We have to go to her – now – quickly!"

I have no idea how I found clothes to pull on, but a sickening, hollow emptiness somehow replaced the tears as I sat in the front seat of the car, while my mother tried to stifle her sobs as she sat behind me. Poor Dad was left behind with Joy, and a neighbour waited in our living room for my friend to arrive, in case Paul woke up. On the way to the hospital we stopped briefly with Philip's parents to give them the awful news that their first grandchild was dead. They followed us soon after.

We travelled in silence for the rest of the short journey.

There was nothing to say.

Ironically, there was no problem parking close to the hospital entrance at such an early hour, and all was quiet as we walked down the seemingly endless corridor to the ward. Irrational feelings of hatred rose to the surface as I blamed this place for taking my daughter: foolish thoughts that quickly disappeared as we entered the ward, where I knew that Cheryl had been lovingly cared for. I guess I just resented having needed it so much over these past ten years!

All was quiet in the semi-darkness of the early hours. No babies were crying. No children coughing. The silence assumed a respectful reverence for the child that had just been lost. The space where her bed had been was now empty. The smiling face of Santa was totally out of place – this was now the Christmas Cheryl would miss. A door opened, and out of a side ward appeared the nurse in charge. She hurried towards me with her arms open wide.

"I'm so sorry," she whispered, as she held me in a warm embrace.

She directed us through a door and we entered the nicely lit side ward. I was speechless as she explained what had happened during Cheryl's last moments, and also her concern that the night sister had made the decision to tell Philip over the phone that Cheryl had died at 12.30 a.m.

But she didn't look dead to me.

Rather, Cheryl was lying propped up on her V-shaped pillow, just like she did every night. And she was so very beautiful – even more than the night I first set eyes on her. Her blonde wavy hair was sitting perfectly, framing her sculptured face, with a complexion that seemed to glow under the lamplight. Her beautiful hands rested on the pink bed cover, displaying neatly trimmed nails – a tribute to the loving preparations the nurse had made when getting Cheryl ready for our arrival.

There was no distress on her face, no fear, and no sign of the week-long struggle she had bravely endured. The nurse had dressed her in a lovely pink and blue cotton dress along with white knee-length lacy socks. What the nurse didn't know was that it was her last birthday dress, bought for her tenth birthday, just four months earlier.

The nurse was still speaking as I was taking in the scene, and, in a surreal way, I heard her relate how she went to change Cheryl's position after midnight.

"I slipped my arms under her, and turned her over," she was explaining. "When she landed on her other side she was gone. My arms were still under her… she was alive on one side – and not on the other. It really was that quick! She didn't deteriorate – honestly. I would have called you if there had been any sign of change."

She struggled to find the words that she needed to explain herself: "It was as if… "

"She was lifted," my mother interrupted.

"That's exactly what I was trying to say!" the nurse exclaimed.

"She was lifted by God, Love," my mum said, trying to be reassuring, as she slipped her arm around my waist.

"Why didn't God allow me to be with her when He came to take her?" I answered, feeling cheated. "Tonight was the first night I had gone home. She was awake earlier – she was getting better!" I protested.

The tender response from my husband caused a momentary silence to fall in the room.

"Cheryl needed you to live, Catherine – she didn't need you to die," he said, trying to help me deal with the guilt and betrayal that was suddenly overwhelming me.

Soon Cheryl was in my arms, and I was so glad of the opportunity we had all had earlier that day to hold her. My tears splashing on her face couldn't awaken her, and my cuddles couldn't cause her bony little body any further pain. She looked at peace, and I knew, as I held her, that she wasn't here any more. Briefly God allowed me to realize that Cheryl was now enjoying the Heaven that I had told her about so many times; now experiencing the new body that had caused so much questioning from Paul. She wouldn't be home for Christmas and yet this would be the first Christmas she would *really* enjoy. The tinsel that the children had attached earlier was still glittering on her cot, its very presence mocking us.

The ward staff were wonderful, as they allowed us so much time with Cheryl. As the hours moved towards morning, other family members were allowed to come and go – to give their beloved grandchild or niece one last cuddle. As I watched my dear dad hold his darling Cheryl, I understood what the term "broken hearted" really meant. And the words that I had rejected earlier that night echoed in my mind: "Be strong, my soul! Lo, here thy God! *He'll bear thee through*; be strong!" And the unspoken prayer of my heart didn't have to travel far, because God was already in the room.

"Help me to be strong, Lord!"

Around 3.30 a.m. on 10 December 1989 I closed the door of the hospital side ward, never to hold my beautiful, brave daughter again. She had been "lifted" into the arms of someone else who loved her, the One who said many years ago: "Let the little children come to me... for of such is the kingdom of Heaven" (Matthew 19:14). And so we headed home to await the dawn, and to tell Paul that his "big" sister had died.

Philip had persuaded me to slip into bed again while we waited for Paul to waken. When Paul had gone to bed the night before, his daddy was still at the hospital. Now Philip was sitting, fully dressed, on the side of the bed, when Paul's little shape walked past our open door to the bathroom. It was 6 a.m. He was always an early bird. As he came back out he looked into our room, and saw his daddy by the dim light of our bedside lamp.

Taking stock of the situation quickly, he asked, "Are you only just home, Daddy? Why have you still got your clothes on?"

Philip beckoned him in.

"Jump in beside Mummy," he said, trying to maintain his composure as he helped Paul into our bed.

Bright child that he was, he guessed something was going on.

"What's wrong, Daddy?" he quizzed, as he pulled the duvet around him against the cold morning air.

Philip's voice seemed remarkably strong as the words came.

"Cheryl died during the night, Paul. She was just too sick, Son, and so God took her to Heaven, where she won't be sick any more."

Paul's little hand went to his face as he smothered a gasp, and in that instant he pushed me away from him. His whole body stiffened and he turned his back on us, cowering, as if we had betrayed him. Meanwhile, I tried to dam back the tears that had formed as I heard Philip use the word "died" to Paul. It really was true... Cheryl was dead.

We gave our wounded son a little space, as he tried to process the kind of news no eight-year-old should have to hear. I wanted to speak – to tell him that it wasn't true. I wanted to protect him from the pain that was starting to invade his young life. But there was nothing I could do. No way could I avoid the truth that two weeks before Christmas, we had lost our daughter, and he had lost his sister. In that moment he didn't even want us to touch him.

"It's OK to be sad, Paul. It's OK to cry," encouraged Philip.

Paul's silence was broken as he quickly turned to face us: his expression now one of anger and betrayal.

"You didn't tell me she was going to die!" he said, accusingly.

Reaching towards him I became defensive, shocked by his accusatory statement.

"But-t-t…" I stammered. "We told you lots of times that Cheryl would die one day, and go to Heaven."

"But you didn't tell me she was going to die *last night*!"

He threw himself into my arms, and the floodgates broke for us all.

"We didn't know she was going to die last night, Sweetheart!" was all I could say.

For a while the three of us lay together wrapped in grief, yet wrapped in love for each other. I wanted to shut the door of that room and never have to leave, but there were other people who loved Cheryl, and as the world was waking up, we needed to break the news to them.

The next few days were a mixture of intense sadness and tangible peace. It has always amazed me how emotions that are poles apart can coexist in the same person. Just as Ireland can experience four seasons in one day, so I experienced anger, sadness, peace and even happiness during the days leading up to the funeral. As people from all over the world prayed for us, we knew the sustaining power of God. In fact, often I was the one who comforted others as they came to our home to offer their sympathy.

Cards, flowers, phone calls, and visitors poured into our home with increasing regularity. With the wonders of technology we talked to people from places as far apart as Belfast and Bolivia. The letters written by doctors, nurses and therapists – who had all played a big part in Cheryl surviving as long as she did – brought us great comfort and pride. Most of them referred to her bravery as she endured difficult procedures, and said how proud they were to have cared for her. One surgeon even apologized that he had been unable to do more to relieve her suffering.

It became obvious that we weren't the only ones who thought that Cheryl Campbell was a very special young lady.

Our home seemed to be constantly full of people, which helped us get through the long days before the funeral. While some people prefer "house private", I feel that we would have missed so much of the comfort and support we received from having our home open to visitors. My kitchen was organized in my absence by a whole team of ministering angels led by both of our own two loving sisters and other friends. People were fed at all times of the day and I was happy to do as I was told for once – and to stay out of the kitchen!

Philip and I were glad, on a few occasions, to be able to escape and go to see Joy, who was still at my parents' home recovering from flu. Holding her brought welcome relief to my empty arms. She was totally unaware of all that was going on, and as she was being well looked after by my parents, I don't think she even missed me. My mum had told this wee mite that Cheryl had gone on to Heaven before her, and Joy responded as she usually did when someone held her and talked to her – she smiled. Joy wouldn't grieve as we would, and for that I was thankful.

In Ireland many families still bring their loved one's

remains home until the funeral. It is both traumatic and enormously comforting. To have Cheryl rest in her small white coffin on top of her own bed, in her own room, was just as it should be, as far as we were concerned. Many of our friends and family were able to have precious time alone with her during those few days. There was just one problem: Paul would happily have brought the entire neighbourhood in to see Cheryl, if we had let him!

Paul had decided that he wanted to go to school until the funeral, and so we agreed that a bit of normality might be good for him. Poor Philip had all the hard jobs to do. So when Paul insisted on going to school the morning after Cheryl died, Philip went with him and spoke to his teacher privately to let her know what had happened. We also wanted to ensure that if Paul became fretful she would contact us. However, if we had known beforehand that the staff at the school would in effect ignore Cheryl's death, I think we would have kept him home. It's sad to think that these professionals, trained in working with children, nevertheless avoided speaking to a child about a sibling's death. Any excuse rings hollow – especially the one that says "We didn't want to make him sad." He was already sad. Instead, the only person to sympathize with our son at school that day was his little classmate, who gave him a neck hug and said: "Hey, Paul, I'm sorry your sister died."

During the time that Paul was at school, Cheryl's remains arrived home. Later he burst in through the front door at the speed of light, and I had to chase upstairs after him to stop him from running into her room! He listened impatiently while changing out of his school uniform, as I tried to prepare him for what he would see.

"Just let's go, Mum!" he said, unwilling to wait any longer.

I was nervous, but Paul was, dare I say it, excited. He had been disappointed when he heard other family members talk about seeing Cheryl the night she died, when he hadn't been given the same opportunity. So now it was his turn, and he wanted to see his sister.

His chattering ceased the moment we entered Cheryl's room.

"She looks like she's sleeping, Mummy," he commented in a forced whisper, glancing at me sideways. He reached out to stroke her face, as he did every time he came home from school, but quickly pulled his hand away.

"She's freezing!" he shouted.

I explained to him that one of the ways we know that the real Cheryl doesn't live in her body any more is that it's very cold. Paul never touched her again. His attention was now diverted to the coffin: my talk about the new body Cheryl now had in Heaven was obviously not as interesting as the object currently holding his sister. He was captivated by it.

Soon he was off to play with his friends at the house next door. Then, ten minutes later, he was back – asking if his friends could see Cheryl and her nice coffin too! (While I believe that what children imagine about death is often worse than the reality, and that it is therefore good to include them in what is going on, a line does need to be drawn.) After discussing the issue of why some people could see Cheryl and perhaps others shouldn't, Paul was told that only those children who knew her well would be allowed to see her – and only with their parents present. As you can imagine, that whittled it down to a few very close friends, whose children said they would like to say goodbye to Cheryl. And for Paul, his days were filled with the see-saw activities of playing outside and quietly slipping in to see his sister from time to time.

The night before the funeral, Paul went in to see Cheryl before he went to bed. It was obvious that he was troubled about something, and so I sat him on my knee to give him the chance to get it off his chest. His response shouldn't have surprised me, as children often think about things that would never cross our minds.

"Will you put her coffin in a plastic bag tomorrow, Mummy?" he said, looking rather worried. "It's such a lovely white coffin, and it will get very dirty if the grave men put muck on it!"

There I was, concerned over what deep, searching question this eight-year-old was going to ask, and all he wanted to know was how we would keep the coffin clean!

After a fitful night's sleep, I woke up very early in the morning and tiptoed into the next room. I didn't want to disturb Philip and Paul earlier than necessary on this most dreaded of days. Today we would say our final farewell to our firstborn – our beautiful, gentle Cheryl. And as I looked at her I didn't know how I would be able to let her leave this house, let alone leave our lives. I spent the next little while talking to her, even though I knew she couldn't hear me. I wanted her to know, once more, how sorry I was that I hadn't been with her when she died. I wanted her to know how much I loved her, and how I would always love her. And I wanted her to know that it would be just a little while before I would be with her again – only then she would be able to talk back to me! In the cool of that room, the emptiness of my heart was filled with a strange sense that she already knew these things.

My mother/daughter time was finally brought to an end as I felt a hand rest on my shoulder. It was Philip.

"Did I waken you?" I asked.

"No," was his simple reply.

"Soon the house will be full. Why don't you have a little time on your own with her, while I go and get ready?"

"OK," was all he said as he took my place on the warm chair.

We had been married for twelve years, and didn't always need a lot of words to communicate what was on our hearts. As I left the room, I could picture his face on the day she was born – that look of pride and delight.

"Please God, help him today," I pleaded, noticing the pain that now accompanied that pride.

The morning passed quickly before the family arrived for the short service at home which was to precede the main funeral service at the church. As the undertaker arrived I had an overwhelming urge to send him away.

"Perhaps he could come another day," I panicked, "it's too soon to let her go!"

He was my friend's father, and that brought me some comfort, as I didn't want just anyone to handle her. I know that in the past he had prayed for her, and so when he hugged me that day and said: "Don't worry, Catherine, I'll look after her," I knew he would.

Looking around the room, I could see that all those who loved both us and Cheryl were there. The arrival of my brother from Germany the previous day had completed the family circle. God had been so good to give both Philip and me such strong, supportive families. Today, of all days, we needed them.

"Be strong, my soul," I whispered.

And God replied: "I'll bear thee through!"

And He kept His promise once more, as I felt myself strangely strengthened during the service, and especially as Cheryl left our home for the last time.

The large church we attended was well filled when we arrived, even though many apologies had been received because people were still affected by the flu epidemic. As I looked around the congregation I was humbled to see so many people gathered to pay tribute to a little girl whom some people might have regarded as a burden to society. Yet Cheryl had touched the lives of many in her ten short years. She had taught us all how to display patience in adversity, to live without grumbling, and even how to see beyond ourselves to the needs of others. Her life was certainly no waste, but rather one that I believe "glorified God" and now she is "enjoying Him for ever", as the Presbyterian catechism would put it.

It seemed so unnatural to stand in church before a small white coffin with a teddy-bear wreath placed on top. Children aren't supposed to die before their parents. It's not how it ought to happen. And as I realized that the white coffin held my *own* child, I felt at that moment it held my heart too.

Good friends bravely took part in the service, and God gave them amazing grace as they did so – especially our close friend (host of the Cloughey circus!) who delivered a wonderful tribute to Cheryl. My heart swelled within me as I heard him speak of all the ways in which her life had blessed and challenged others. Every now and then Paul would glance up at me, or tap my arm and give a little reassuring smile, agreeing with all that was being said. The minister who had dedicated Cheryl ten years earlier returned to speak at her funeral. He chose a phrase from Jeremiah 15:9 as his text.

"Her sun has gone down while it was yet day."

Within that powerful sermon was the most comforting of thoughts: "The sun sets on one horizon that it might rise in another!" he declared.

What a beautiful description of death – setting on one horizon, while simultaneously rising in another. And I remembered what the nurse had said a few short days before: "On one side she was alive, and on the other side – 'she had been lifted!'"

Cheryl had had a seamless passing indeed.

The service was over, and as our family turned to follow Cheryl's small coffin as it left the church the most amazing thing happened.

My gaze was fixed on the coffin as it was carried down the aisle. An overwhelming feeling of pride came over me as I thought of Cheryl, and God gave me what I can only describe as a beautiful picture of what was happening to her. (I'm not into visions, or the like, but I believe this picture was God, in His mercy, allowing me to know that all was well with our daughter.)

I clearly saw Cheryl running up a long path towards Jesus, who had His arms opened wide. He was bending down towards her, and as He scooped her up and swung her around, I heard Him say unmistakably: "Well done, Pet. You've been such a good girl!"

It came in a flash and was gone just as quickly, but in that instant I knew that God had welcomed her home… and that He was pleased with her. She had received the glorious welcome she deserved!

I didn't go to the cemetery, where the sleet of that cold December day lashed the mourners relentlessly, and where God answered my prayers for Philip, and gave him help as they lowered his lovely child into the dark earth.

Children grieve very differently from the way adults do, and depending on their age and circumstances, their grief can even differ from one child to another. The well-documented stages of grief – shock, denial, anger, sadness and acceptance – are also experienced by children. It is therefore very important to watch for changes in behaviour that may appear to have nothing to do with the child's loss, but which may in fact have everything to do with it. Regression to behaviour associated with a younger age is the most common form of non-verbal communication children can use when seeking attention for their loss. Often children cannot explain their behaviour; they genuinely have no idea what's wrong with them. Also there is no accepted length of time for each of the stages of grief, or what order they come in – apart from acceptance, which is last… unless the other stages are revisited.

One of the best ways to help our children grieve is in preparation. Not merely by preparing them for a death, because not all deaths are expected: some are very sudden. The best form of preparation is in having a good relationship with our children. They will not find it easy to talk over the sadness in their hearts if they have not previously been used to talking to us about everyday issues.

It's true that not all children are talkers, but all children can be taught to engage in conversation if we persevere. We need to learn to use open-ended questions from the time they are very young. Getting them used to sharing things will form the good habit of openness within a family. And it will pay dividends, because there will come a day when our children will need to talk, and we want it to be us they will talk to.

We were very fortunate: Paul was always a talker. He could speak in sentences before he was brave enough to walk. And he knew from his first class that his mummy would never be satisfied with "OK" as the answer to the question: "How did school go today?" So we talked to him about everything that was appropriate, while he found it easier just to tell us everything! That way he knew we cared about every area of his life, and then as he grew older it was less difficult for him to open up when he needed to.

Well, that was the theory, and you know what they say about theories – they don't always work, as I found out.

Shortly after Cheryl died I was feeling very sorry that Paul had no "normal" siblings, and I came out with one of those throwaway comments. Not really expecting an answer from my eight-year-old son I said: "I'm sure it hasn't always been easy for you, son, having two disabled sisters?"

Without changing his position, he replied: "It's just hard when other boys call you names, and say 'You're a plastic spastic like your sisters!'"

I nearly fell off my chair!

"Who said that?" I demanded. "Why didn't you tell me about this?" I went on in my shock, hardly giving Paul time to reply.

"They're just not nice boys, Mummy, and anyway, my sisters aren't plastic spastics! What do they know?"

He appeared unperturbed, yet I knew it must have hurt him at the time, or he wouldn't have brought it up even now. For him it was over, but for me it was yet another hurt he had endured because of his sisters.

In general, we were able to talk with Paul about most things, but usually only when he was ready. It would be Christmas in less than two weeks, and for now that was what occupied most of his thinking. Because I am a fairly organized person, some of the Christmas gift shopping had already been done before Cheryl went into hospital. The rest was left undone, apart from one day when Philip took me out to escape the house for a little while. We wandered around a large shop, amazed to see the rest of the world carrying on with its business as if nothing had happened.

Something in me wanted to yell at the shoppers: "Don't you realize that our little girl is dead?"

It felt unreal to me that "normal" things could be going on while we were in a state of deep sadness.

I love Christmas. I always have, and always will. Not merely because of decorations, gifts, and family visits: I love Christmas because it spells hope. It reminds me that God poured hope into a world that had no hope, spiritually speaking. Every one of us is hopeless because of our sin; separated from a holy God, not only for now but also for eternity. Without God, the meaning of life evades us, and we are denied a personal relationship with the only One who can fill up the empty places with His peace and purpose.

St Augustine said: "Thou hast made us for Thyself, and our hearts are restless, 'til they find their rest in Thee."

However, on that very first Christmas, God set about putting the hope back into our lives. By sending His Son Jesus into this world to be our Saviour, God once more made it possible for us to have a relationship with our Creator through repentance and faith. Hope for the hopeless was restored – that's why I love Christmas!

Now, on this saddest of all Christmases, I was still preparing to celebrate – not merely because I had other children, but because Christmas spelled *hope* to me in bigger letters than ever. Without the Saviour, my loss would be totally pointless. He it was who gave me not only the hope, but also the assurance that He makes no mistakes; that He understands my pain, and is with me in it; that He welcomed Cheryl into Heaven, and that one day I will be with her again. How could I not celebrate the season of the year that reminds us of the kind of hope that only God can give?

Undoubtedly Christmas would be different from now on, but whereas happiness depends on happenings, joy does not. And so Christmas came – with much sadness, and many tears, yet with joy in the experience of God's love surrounding me.

I even managed some smiles as we watched Paul enjoy his somewhat smaller-than-usual pile of presents. And Philip presented me with a beautiful photograph album of Cheryl, probably the most precious Christmas present I have ever been given. He had lovingly put it together late at night, after I had gone to bed, in order to surprise me. It was his way of ensuring her little face was still with us on Christmas morning, as the album, with Cheryl's photo on the front, was sitting in her chair waiting for us to arrive.

What a surprise! In the space of ten short nights Philip had been able to retrieve enough photographs to celebrate her life in a most beautiful way.

We also used the album as a conversation starter with Paul, whenever we looked at it together. He loved looking at the pictures, and we did spend some time laughing too, especially at the captions Philip had written under them. Different pictures would bring out different memories. When looking at one of Cheryl and Joy lying at either end of the settee, like a pair of bookends, Paul suddenly said: "Mum, do you remember the night Cheryl smiled?"

I certainly did. And the two of us discussed together the delight her last smile had given us, just months before she died. After she was very ill with measles around the age of eight, Cheryl had rarely, if ever, smiled. It was medically attributed to further brain damage caused by the measles virus. One night the girls were both lying in their pyjamas at either end of the settee (just like in the picture), when Joy took a fit of the giggles. Paul loved to hear Joy laugh, and he was keeping the laughter going by tickling her knees. I was about to break up the teasing when he suddenly announced: "Look, Mummy, Cheryl is smiling – she's *really* smiling!" True enough, Cheryl was actually responding to the raucous giggling and laughter in the room. For at least a minute the big, broad smile never left Cheryl's face. It was one of those precious heavenly gifts that lifted our spirits, and that day looking at the photograph Paul remembered it.

"I'll never forget it, Mummy – the night Cheryl smiled!"

Paul swung back into his busy weekly programme as an eight-year-old. School and friends, along with gymnastics, Boys' Brigade, and music lessons filled his days. There wasn't much time to grieve, although he undoubtedly missed his sister. And coming home to Joy helped to fill the gap left by Cheryl. He would fuss over her, read to her, and tickle her incessantly.

As a child Paul was never really interested in having pets, but he did have goldfish. There were always two of them swimming around in the bowl in his room. What he didn't know for a long time, however, was the number of times that he returned home from school to a replacement. Goldfish don't live very long, and so if one died, or was near to it, we would get one to replace it while Paul was out at school. He usually didn't notice, and so for a long time we avoided him having to deal with a floating-fish situation! Then one day, a month after Cheryl died, I noticed that Spock looked a bit "off", but then I promptly forgot all about it.

Paul arrived home from school as chirpy as ever, and went upstairs to change. Within a few minutes the sound of wailing could be heard throughout the house.

"Oh no," I thought, "the goldfish… I forgot about the goldfish!"

I ran into the hall to see our distressed son standing at the top of the stairs, goldfish bowl in hand.

"It's not fair, Mummy!" he sobbed. "My goldfish *and* my sister are dead! What am I going to do? Why did my goldfish have to die too?"

I ran upstairs to comfort him (and to prevent him from dropping the bowl, whose water was splashing all over the floor with his shaking). His reaction to the dead fish was way out of proportion, but experiencing another loss was simply too much for him to bear. It took a long time to settle him, and I'm sure the distress was really more about his sister than his goldfish.

However, one lovely thing about grief in young children is that they seem to have the ability to move through it more quickly than adults. One summer's day, six months later, we were returning from a visit to the cemetery, and I could see Paul in the rear-view mirror. He was unusually quiet, and so I asked him what was wrong.

"I've got something to tell you, Mummy," he said, "but I don't want it to make you sad."

"That's OK, Paul," I replied, rather puzzled, "just tell me anyway."

"I've decided not to be sad any more about Cheryl," he remarked, while changing his position to watch my reaction.

"Oh!" I said, rather surprised. "And why is that?" I asked, while trying to keep my eyes on the road.

"I'm not going to be sad because Cheryl is in Heaven, and she won't have to be sick *ever again*! And I'm glad about that. You're not cross with me, are you, Mummy?"

I could see his troubled expression in the mirror. He genuinely didn't want to hurt me, yet he had worked out in his young heart that Heaven *was* better for Cheryl, and so it was really quite logical – he wouldn't be sad any more!

And my heart melted.

10

Living Again

anuary came, as January does, with short dark days and heavily laden skies. Staying-at-home weather suited me perfectly, when at least the sunshine wasn't around to mock my mood. I went out when it was expected of me, but the winter months gave me a more natural opportunity to hide away from people whenever possible.

As I watched Paul return to school after the Christmas break, I envied him somewhat. A child's ability not to dwell on anything for too long was a trait I greatly desired, as the depth of my sadness was relentless. Joy had also returned to school, having recovered from her bout of flu. Filling the hours was not easy for me, as my decision-making was poor. Often even the simplest of tasks would take a long time to perform, or be left undone. Visitors were also treated with a mixture of responses – either welcome relief or reluctant endurance.

As expected, the number of visitors decreased after the funeral, but we were still well cared for by our large group of friends and church family. Professional visitors continued to call to see Joy, but I had a sneaking suspicion that their visits were to check on how I was doing as well.

One day a member of the Children's Hospital bereavement team arrived for a visit, and as I looked at the young woman sitting across the room from me, I both admired and was puzzled by her. Her job on the hospital's social work team was to counsel families who had had a child die at the hospital. I couldn't think of a more distressing form of employment than visiting families in the early stages of grief. She, however, seemed relaxed, thoughtful, and was obviously very good at her job.

She was a good listener. In fact she said nothing at all for a long time, letting me tell her about Cheryl and how she had died. I appreciated the opportunity to talk to someone who wasn't close and, therefore, who couldn't be hurt by what I said. At the same time it was strange to talk about Cheryl to someone who had never met her. There was, however, one thing she said to me that didn't make sense at the time, but which I have proved down through the years to be absolutely true.

"Catherine," she said, "your life will never be the same again – *but it doesn't have to be worse.*"

"What nonsense!" were the words shouting back at her in my head, words I was glad she couldn't hear.

She went on to say that it *is* possible to live again after the death of a child, but that it would take a lot of readjustment.

"One day you won't feel as bad as you do today, and that will be the start of planning for the future again."

"Future! What future?" was my silent retort.

Talk of support groups and further counselling just didn't grab me. I was already surrounded by lots of people who provided me with all I needed. That is, apart from the one thing I wanted so badly: Cheryl's presence.

Whenever I could summon up either the energy or the motivation, my days were filled with plenty to keep me busy. I had a bright, bubbly eight-year-old son and a darling daughter of four, who required my attention twenty-four/seven. Having Joy meant that my connection with the same doctors, therapists and teacher was unbroken, and there was a certain comfort in maintaining that contact. They had all played such a large part in our lives for such a long time. Unfortunately I was finding no pleasure in anything I did; even nursing Joy just made me want Cheryl more.

My heart was empty, yet at the same time it felt like a lead weight. Fake smiles became the mask I hid behind, and as the world moved on, I wanted to go back – back to the days when Cheryl was there at every turn.

Grief, I discovered, is cruel and illogical.

"Sure, you have two other children who need you," some folk would say.

But the child I longed for most at that time was the one who didn't need me any more.

Grief is also very lonely and selfish. It condemns you to solitary confinement; it makes you feel as if no one else is suffering like you, even though there are others who are grieving just as much. Yet you just can't see it! I began to look on grief like a great big coat that I picked up every day and chose to wear, not daring to dispose of it in case the one I was grieving for might think I didn't care any more. Grief becomes your hiding place, but it doesn't keep you safe. Instead, it seems to shut the door on hope. And worst of all, grief becomes your accuser, as it is fertile ground in which feelings of guilt can flourish.

Guilt was my enemy, dogging my footsteps.

"If only I hadn't left her that night!" I would repeat to myself over and over again. "If only I had gone back to the ward after Philip returned home!"

"How could I have left her alone to die?" was the accusing question that became the belt that fastened the coat of grief tighter around me.

Yet from the depths of my soul came a whisper that I

chose to ignore: "She was *not* alone, Catherine, *I* was with her – just as I promised you I would be."

The distant voice of God was held at bay by my distress and anger: anger that He had not allowed me to be with my child when I felt she needed me the most; anger at the thought of caring for her for ten long years, only to be denied those last precious moments with her. But anger directed at God is not only sinful, it is also destructive.

For the previous ten years I had experienced the love and support of the God of Heaven. Often He had turned my despair into hope… my disappointment into peace… my sorrow into joy. There had been special times when His presence was so real, I was sure that if I had stretched out my hand, I could have touched Him. Now I kept at a distance the only One who could give "the oil of joy for mourning, the garment of praise for the spirit of heaviness" (Isaiah 61:3).

Instead, I tried to assuage my guilt and comfort my soul by attempting to be as close to Cheryl as I could be. So every day I made the twenty-minute drive to visit her grave, while each Saturday night I would sit by her empty bed, trying to make up for the Saturday night I had left her alone to die.

And still I had no peace.

Instead I allowed grief and guilt to do the work of the enemy of my soul – to torment and accuse me.

And so the months rolled on with very few people aware of the battle I was waging, and the awful devastation that was wreaking havoc in my life. I had become an accomplished actor, putting on a good front and accepting the readjustments that had to be made – to good effect. After all, my husband was a preacher, and it wouldn't do to let people see how the preacher's wife had all but crumbled on the inside!

"Isn't it better for her," folk would remark. "And it takes the burden from you as well," they would add, assuming that Cheryl's death was some kind of relief for us. My response would be a false smile, accompanied by inward anger.

"Why should the death of my child be any different from another?" I questioned silently. "Just because she was disabled, that doesn't mean we miss her any less than a *normal* child!"

Joy's fifth birthday came in July, six days before what would have been Cheryl's eleventh. All the family gathered for the party, only this time Paul had just one set of candles to blow out. He had decorated the room with hand-painted banners, and struck up "Happy Birthday" on his keyboard when I carried her downstairs earlier that morning. I could see that his effort was about more than Joy's birthday: he wanted a happy Mummy too! And I tried very hard to be all things to all people, but the sadness refused to lighten, and God seemed to be silent.

We were careering towards Cheryl's first anniversary, and all I could think about was how wrong that social worker had been. Life *was* worse since Cheryl died, and as far as I was concerned, it could *never* be the same again! For ten years most of my waking moments had been bound up in that child. My days were organized by caring for her. Even my spiritual life was greatly affected by her. I had learned so much about God because of her. His word had taken on a new dimension in my life during those years. I had relished the time I spent in His presence, and enjoyed the company of God in a way I had not previously experienced, and I believed it was all because of Cheryl. For eight years I had even crossed the country speaking at ladies' meetings, encouraging women to trust God with the most difficult circumstances of their lives.

But since she left me, I had felt spiritually bereft. In a strange way I was equating my relationship with God to Cheryl alone. And now she was gone, I didn't seem to have any reason left to live. I was never suicidal: I just felt that I would never truly live again, now that she was gone. As far as I could see there could be no happiness, no fulfilment, no purpose left in my life without her.

I was convinced that I should learn to accept this form of existence, while at the same time I knew deep down that God was working on my behalf. In this "dark night of the soul" I began to realize that the answer to my need lay in giving up my anger, and trusting in the One who had never let me down before.

So I returned to prayer. Not the God-bless-the-whole-world type of praying that I had been fooling myself with, believing that I was OK spiritually because I managed a few verses of the Bible and a few words with God before I closed my eyes at night. No, I returned to honest communication with my Saviour. No more trying to fool Him – as if I could! I simply told Him how I felt. I let the anger, the bitterness, the intense sadness and the feelings of hopelessness all spill out of my broken heart.

I knew He would know what to do with it all, and with the honesty came a glimmer of light breaking through the dark clouds that were my daily companions. Genuine smiles started to cross my face. Real enjoyment in my children began to permeate my days. The weight in my chest seemed very slightly lighter, and the whispers of God were remaining for longer, as I repented of my anger towards Him. And every day the request of my heart was always the same.

"Please, God, show me if there is any reason left for me to live!"

God's response came one quiet Sunday afternoon. Philip was out, Paul was at Sunday school, and Joy was having her afternoon nap. I always loved Sunday, as we had made it our practice to honour the Sabbath by keeping it special. It was not out of legalism, but out of a genuine love for the Saviour that we decided early in our marriage to make Sunday different. Watching television, shopping and the like were kept for other days, while we aimed Sunday's activities at worshipping the One who had given His all for us. It has never been a chore; rather, it has been a delight, and particularly on that Sunday, almost a year after Cheryl's passing.

As Joy slept, I put a music tape in the hi-fi and started to read while it quietly played in the background. I closed my Bible and prayed as I had on so many other occasions before. My prayers were very selfish, so full of *me*, and as I finished, my heart's cry was still the same.

"God, please show me if there is any reason left for me to live!"

The tape had continued to play while I was praying, and as I blew my nose and dried my eyes, I could hear God's very clear reply to the incessant questioning of my heart. A young woman who had been crippled in a diving accident was singing:

> *I've finally found the reason for living,*
> *It's in giving every part of my life to Him,*
> *All that I do, every word that I say,*
> *I'll be giving it all back to Him…*
> *For…*
> *We were the reason that He gave His life,*
> *We were the reason that He suffered and died.*
> *To a world that was lost He gave all He could*
> * give*

To show us the reason to live…
He is my reason to live!

As the song finished I sat dumbfounded at the direct answer to my direct question, and God continued to speak clearly to this seeking, grief-stricken mother.

"Catherine," He said, as the music faded, "to be a good wife and mother is right and proper, but it is not to be your reason to live. *I* am your reason to live."

I was taken back to the Cross, where "To a world that was lost, He gave all He could give to show us the reason to live." I knew in that instant, as I pictured Jesus suffering on that Roman cross for me, that *He* was to be my reason to live!

In this world of constant change, God does not change. In this world of suffering, only God can bring true peace. In this world where people cause us disappointment, God is our fulfilment. In this world where promises are easily broken, only God will *always* keep His. In a world where those we love may leave us, only God can and will stay with us for ever.

There is no doubt that, because of Cheryl, I had walked with God in ways I never thought possible. Now I realized that Cheryl's death didn't mean that I was prevented from walking with God again.

In that room on that particular day I had a choice to make. God had shown me that there *was* a reason left for me to live, and that reason was Him. Was I going to choose to live for Him, or was I going to choose to wrap my coat of grief closer around me and stay in the darkness? At that point, I knew it was up to me.

"Pain is inevitable, but misery is optional," is a Barbara Johnston quote that I had used many times when giving talks to women. Now it was my turn to practise what I preached. Was I going to choose misery over a renewed walk with the One who could have me stand under the rainbow again? Reminding myself that God had never promised me a life without pain, but rather His presence in it, I slipped from the chair to my knees, and made Him my reason to live.

The quietness of that special moment with God was suddenly interrupted by happy chatter as Philip and Paul returned home. Paul ran to me, but stopped on seeing the red nose and swollen eyes he had seen so many times before.

"Are you sad, Mummy?" he questioned, as he threw his arms around me for a tight squeeze.

"No, Paul, I'm not," I replied honestly. "Mummy is happier than she has been for a long time!"

"Yeah!" he shouted, "I'm so glad, Mummy, 'cause I don't like to see you sad!"

The valley of the shadow of death referred to in Psalm 23 was a place we were meant to "walk through", but for almost a year I had pitched my tent in it. As I started living again, I was helped out of my valley by an unseen hand. I was soon to discover that I could weep without feeling despair. Sadness was no longer accompanied by hopelessness, but instead by the knowledge that we don't sorrow in the same way as others who have no hope. (See 1 Thessalonians 4:13.) I therefore determined, with God's help, not to allow guilt to spoil the promise that one day I would see my lovely daughter again. The missing-you days still rolled over my life with regularity, but never again was I to experience the absolute devastation of the previous year.

Jesus became my ultimate focus – my reason to live. He had my heart: completely. I knew I could trust Him with today, tomorrow, and every other day after that, as long as I kept my eyes fixed on Him. The sun began to shine in my life again, breaking up the dark clouds, and revealing the beauty of His rainbow once more.

I thought about Cheryl every single day, but there were now some days when I could remember her without pain. I started to look forward to going out for lunch with friends; no longer afraid of whom we might meet, or what they might say. Visiting Joy in the same classroom that she had once shared with Cheryl became enjoyable again, rather than one more place where Cheryl was missing. Joining in games and outings with Paul and Philip brought fun into my life once more. Fun! Now there's a word I didn't think I would ever use again!

The following summer, when Paul was ten years old, we even crossed the Atlantic for the first time. We had an amazing holiday in Canada for three whole weeks, while Joy stayed at home, being spoiled by her Granny and Granda. The funny thing about that holiday was that by the end of it, Joy had more of a suntan than we did, as Canada experienced its worst summer weather on record! Still, the memories we gained were far more important than the weather.

And I started to believe that what the social worker had said was actually true: My life would never be the same again, but it didn't have to be worse.

11

A Special Place

I was sorry when the Department of Education decided to leave the word "Special" out of the names of schools for children with severe learning difficulties. They really are special places, and different from the normal establishments we know as school. This type of school does not merely facilitate academic learning, but rather it meets a variety of needs represented in its pupils.

For children like Joy, a high staff/pupil ratio is provided because of the amount of personal care that is required. The children in the special unit need to be fed and changed, cuddled and comforted, alongside a tailored programme of "education", which some educationalists might not even regard as worthy of the name. Sensory stimulation is a widely used tool to encourage response from the children, which in turn receives praise equal to any prize-day tribute for exam success. For parents like us, a smile from our child at the appropriate time can mean as much as any A*!

With that in mind, Joy's classroom was fitted out with all kinds of accoutrements. There was a large bubble tube, standing taller than any of the classroom staff, surrounded by a cushioned seat. If their joints allowed it, the children could sit astride, with arms held around the amazing piece of equipment, while colourful bubbles floated past and the whole thing vibrated, tickling as it did so.

Walking across the room was like hiking through a forest of glittering, tinkling vines, stretching from ceiling to floor, evoking smiles and giggles from the little pupils who were placed on floor mats or in special seats. Happy music, moving lights, tactile toys and a number of pairs of loving hands were used daily to bring stimulation and delight.

And there was no such thing as missing out on out-of-doors activities just because you couldn't walk. Sometimes I was exhausted just reading what Joy had been up to during the day, especially in the summer. Trips to the seaside with toes splashed in the tide; stroking rabbits at the fun farm; picnicking in the park. There was never a dull moment in Joy's class – even the mums were invited to coffee and cake from time to time.

The class size in a special unit is kept very small, accommodating from five to seven children with profound disabilities. As the staff work hands-on for long periods of time with these extremely dependent children, the children become more than mere pupils. It is natural therefore that the staff forge strong, affectionate links with them, and often with their families as well. Next to the child's family, the teacher probably spends more time with the child than anyone else during their lifetime.

That fact only hit me after Cheryl died.

As a grieving mother, it was easy for me to forget that there were other important people in my child's life, all of whom had lavished substantial amounts of time, effort, and even love on her. They too had watched our brave child struggle and suffer, all the while developing a close relationship with her over the years. When she died, they also felt the loss very keenly. I became aware of this because Joy was taught by Lillian Hill, the same teacher as Cheryl, which meant my contact with her remained unbroken.

When I visited the school I saw how much Lillian and her staff missed Cheryl. They were very professional, of course, as they tried not to upset me by their comments, yet it was obvious that they too enjoyed the opportunity to indulge in reminiscing. Looking around that small class of beautiful children, I knew that Cheryl would not be the only one they would have to say goodbye to. I felt enormous gratitude towards Lillian, who was the only member of staff who stayed year-on-year with this special class: gratitude for her commitment, as teaching these children was more than a job to her, and gratitude that she allowed herself to love each of the children in her care – even though it would prove costly. Within about a year of Cheryl's death, Lillian lost another of her young pupils.

Then early in 1993, all the parents of her pupils received an invitation to her home to have a meeting with her husband, Tom, to discuss our views about the concept of a children's hospice. Even as a nurse, I had never heard of a hospice for children before. The term "hospice" conjured up thoughts of cancer and death – certainly nothing that I felt was relevant to our children. In addition, I knew that the cancer unit in the Children's Hospital already gave remarkable care to children with cancer, and to their families. However, because I held Lillian in such esteem, I decided to go and see what it was all about, while Philip stayed at home that evening to look after Joy.

I don't remember having met Tom Hill before that night. First impressions were of a man who appeared a little nervous, which is no wonder really, since he was surrounded by a group of mostly women who were already acquainted with each other to some degree. He was very welcoming, making us feel at home in his large sitting room. His quiet, gentle demeanour portrayed reassurance as he started to explain why he had asked us to come. After talking about how he had watched his wife grieve first for Cheryl and then for Peter, he found himself asking the question: "If Lillian feels this way, how on earth must the families feel?"

He continued by explaining how he had always loved hearing about this group of children, and how he had started to nip into the classroom to meet them. As he did so, he began to realize all that was involved in their care on a daily basis.

"Soon I found myself asking Lillian more and more about what help was available for these families," he went on to say. "Who looks after the children when mum is sick? How do they manage to get away on holiday? What about the other children in the family?"

Here was a man who was asking all the right questions, I thought, as I listened to him express genuine concern for families with whom he had no personal connection – a rare quality indeed! In a very short time Tom had won over his listeners by his understanding heart, which was not surprising: Tom and Lillian had a son of their own with disabilities.

At that time Tom was the administrative director of the Northern Ireland Hospice, a facility providing care for terminally ill adults. As we sipped tea, he told us of a recent trip that he had just taken to England, where an opportunity was given for the delegates to visit a children's hospice. His eyes lit up as he told us of his surprise to discover that the place was full of children – just like those in Lillian's class. After that informative visit on providing care for life-limited children Tom was a driven man –

driven by the thought that a much better service could be provided for the Joys and Jonathans of this world.

The words "life-limited" rested uneasily in my heart. Cheryl's death had forced me to recognize that one day Joy would also die, but some of these parents had probably never thought of *their* child as being included in that scenario – at least not until now. There was no doubt that respite care was all but impossible to obtain for some of our children who required tube feeding, and the like; no doubt that our area had no paediatric community nursing service at all; no doubt that there was no provision for any of our children to die at home, whenever the time came.

But the thought of looking after our children in a hospice was still something hard to understand – that is, until Tom showed us the video.

On the television screen we were taken to a beautiful place that looked more like a big home than a hospital. Members of staff wore ordinary clothes, and the bedrooms had adjoining rooms for family members. There was a huge table in the open-plan kitchen, where everyone, children, parents and staff alike, met together at meal times as one big family. Parents spoke of how the hospice had supported all their family, including siblings and grandparents. Staff explained simply that a children's hospice provided care for children who had conditions which would probably prevent them reaching adulthood – hence the term "life-limited".

The service provided the elusive respite that could keep carers sane, and home visits for support and advice in-between stays at the hospice. But the part that interested me most was that they gave families the choice of where their children would spend their last days. At that time there was no choice for us. Our children would die in hospital, because there was no support available for those of us who wanted our child to die in the familiar surroundings of home, or in a peaceful hospice.

We all watched in silence for the twelve or so minutes it took to watch the recorded presentation. What we were looking at was revolutionary! It was hope-generating. It showed us the kind of place we thought existed only in our dreams. Everything Tom had said before was clearly brought into focus. A children's hospice was a place where children and their families could get on with living, for whatever time they had, and a place that could help them with the dying.

Before I could speak, someone else had said what was on all our minds.

"Can we not have one of these hospices for *our* children?"

Tom's delight at our positive response was obvious, as we all tried to speak our approval at the same time.

"It will take time to make a proper case to present to the Hospice Council," he interrupted. "We will have to prove the need for a children's hospice here in Northern Ireland. It will involve a lot of work and effort, but if you give me your support I'm willing to try."

Each member of that small group of parents had been used to hard work. Often we had had to fight for the services our children needed – even, at times, against the odds. So there and then we asked Tom Hill to start the process, and we would back him to the hilt!

None of us realized in 1993 how long it would take to realize those dreams.

The Council quickly dismissed the first approach Tom made, requesting consideration of a service for life-limited children. But Tom Hill was a visionary, a dream maker, and a risk taker. As he gathered more and more information about the growing worldwide children's hospice movement, he was encouraged to persevere. Added to which, there were a number of little faces etched on his mind that kept him going when lesser men might have given up.

So month after month, he added the case for a children's hospice to the agenda, slowly wearing down the resistance of those who felt that they had enough to do running an adult service. And at last a sub-committee was formed to look at Tom's proposal, and to provide more information for the Hospice Council. The first hurdle had been crossed, and the families were delighted.

Meetings with the relevant children's professionals were set up to discuss the current poor provision for life-limited children in the Province of Northern Ireland. Evidence of need was an essential component if we were to move forward. We, along with other parents, told our personal stories of yawning gaps in service provision, but none of these cash-strapped authorities was either prepared or willing to initiate the changes that were needed. Instead they were only too glad that a voluntary organization might do their job for them.

The hard facts about the numbers of children who could benefit from such a service were provided by paediatricians and GPs, which helped to bolster our case. The sub-committee was eventually won over, and they agreed to look into it further. In 1997 it was my privilege to accompany them, on behalf of the families, to a visit to Acorns, a children's hospice in Birmingham. What an amazing day that was! On our return, the sub-committee recommended the setting up of a Children's Hospice Project to fund the building and running of a children's hospice service for Northern Ireland. It was four years since Tom's initial proposal.

The families were elated.

By that time Philip and I thought it would be too late for Joy, who was twelve years old, to benefit from such a service. However, we threw our weight behind it for all the families who would follow after us. In our view, there was no one better than Tom Hill to direct the project, and we were delighted when his appointment was made official.

In the mercy of God, Joy was still alive to attend the official launch of the Project on 28 February 1998. Sister Frances Dominica, an Anglican nun and founder of the worldwide Children's Hospice Movement, launched the project, and it was our privilege to share the platform with her that day. (Her work at Helen House, in Oxford, remains the Gold Standard for children's hospice care throughout the world.) It was a nerve-wracking, exciting and proud day, as we were interviewed by reporters from television, radio, and newspapers, all wanting to know about Joy (and her sister before her), and how a hospice would change the lives of families like ours.

So began a whirlwind year of speaking at events, and representing what the media affectionately termed "the founding families". Photographs of Joy, Jonathan, Natasha, Rebecca, Nicole, Ashleigh and Ellen were seen on billboards, newspapers, concert programmes, and collecting boxes all over Northern Ireland, as the people of our little Province took the children to their hearts and went into a fund-raising frenzy! Nothing like it had been seen before or since.

Joy's health was deteriorating, but we continued our involvement, allowing the public on occasion to see what we would have preferred to keep private. Our belief that people needed to know what caring for a life-limited child was *really* all about could sometimes result in intrusion, misrepresentation and hurt. But in the majority of cases it produced an outpouring of support and love from every corner of the Province. People from all backgrounds and persuasions got together to build a children's hospice. Even Prince Charles added his support by meeting with the families at a special event in the spring of 1998.

All the founding families were involved in one way or another, and I pay tribute to them for the personal sacrifices they made in order to see the children's hospice become a reality. The project would have floundered were it not for the determination and willingness of seven families to make public their personal heartache.

As for the children, I take my hat off to all of them. You are special, every one! Thanks go to you, Natasha, Ashleigh, and Ellen – and also to the memory of Joy, Jonathan, Rebecca and Nicole, not forgetting Cheryl and Peter, whose deaths provided the momentum for the whole project. These are the unsung heroes of a service that came into being in 2001, enabling families with a life-limited child to enjoy the provision that exists today.

Sadly, however, as with many noble causes, sin can often spoil what is good. Our dear friend Tom Hill did indeed fulfil his dream, but did so ultimately at great cost to himself, because of the ill-founded actions of others. Our heartfelt thanks go to Tom, without whom there might never have been a children's hospice in Northern Ireland.

12

Wriggly Giggly Joy

If ever a name suited anyone, Joy's name suited her.

She was such a pleasant child. Our family photograph albums testify to that. While Cheryl lost her smile when she was very young, Joy continued to charm everyone by the one thing that she could do well: smile! Paul loved to read to her from books that had accompanying silly sounds, which without fail would bring a smile to her face. He would scoop her up in his arms, cuddling her close, while balancing a book across both of their knees. Joy was his little sister and stayed little enough to always enjoy her brother's embraces.

She also loved music to be playing around her, even though she was unable to locate where the sound was actually coming from. While her visual response was difficult to assess, it was obvious that she could almost hear the proverbial grass growing! Silence, however, was the time she would use to exercise her own vocal cords, usually with searching grunting noises. I guess if translation was available, it would amount to: "Is anybody there? Do you not realize I'm here?" The "pick-me-up" call was most often used in the middle of the night, as Joy knew very little about sleep.

Neither did she have any idea how to distinguish between the differing sounds that she heard. She would react to a stern shout in the room in exactly the same way as she would to a lullaby: she would simply smile. Her startle reflex had left her early on in her development, and very few noises seemed to frighten or alarm her, except for one: the sound of a trumpet. Whereas loud noises often made her giggle, the trumpet always caused her lip to drop and tears to come. That greatly distressed Paul, who had been learning to play the trumpet from the age of ten. His little sister just couldn't appreciate his gift. Instead he had to stick to playing the piano for her, and make sure the trumpet sounds were kept at a safe distance.

Every Christmas and birthday Joy received gifts of noisy or tactile toys to encourage these responses that brought us so much pleasure.

Those early years after Cheryl's death were possibly the nearest we came to a normal family life. Joy's health remained fairly good and we were able to take part in all the usual extended family experiences. We particularly enjoyed visits from my sister's family, and her young boys loved to spend time with their cousins Paul and Joy. Paul even taught them where to tickle Joy so that she would giggle for them. Much to their delight, it worked every time, while our ripples of laughter fuelled the response from Joy.

The highlight of every year was Hillcroft's Christmas production, where every child in the school was given a part in the Christmas play. These events were both hilarious and emotionally draining. At times some of the more able children had us in stitches with a sudden self-interpretation of their roles. On one such occasion Baby Jesus was propelled across the room by a disgruntled visiting shepherd!

Even Lillian's class had their part to play and Joy had been an angel, a tree and a woodland animal at various times. What a delight. Yet with each passing year you could identify the children who were getting weaker, and notice the absence of those who were no longer there. But without doubt those few hours were memory makers of epic proportions.

Getting out of doors was equally important, in spite of the amount of "stuff" that had to be transported for Joy. Granda, however, had a much simpler mode of transport: two feet. Sometimes this doting grandfather referred to Joy as if she were something akin to a young seedling.

"Put Joy's coat on," he would say over the phone. "I'm coming down to take her out for a walk – she needs a wee bit of air."

Even in the depths of winter the request could not be put off.

"Just wrap her up well… the air is good for her."

And this wonderful man would walk the streets with his darling Joybells, as he would affectionately call her. Everybody in the neighbourhood seemed to know the man who pushed the strange buggy holding the little girl. And Joy loved it.

Joy was easy to love.

From a young age, Paul was into making things that usually included lights of all descriptions: he once made Joy an amazing flashing coloured light box to try to stimulate her sight. We all enjoyed it, even if we were unsure as to how much of it Joy could actually see. Even as a teenager Paul loved her unashamedly, and as her big brother he always made time for her.

Joy's giggling did start to concern me, even though the whole family seemed to derive such pleasure from it. She would throw her head back, and out would come a real belly laugh that set everyone within earshot into peals of laughter. The only problem was that we could stop laughing when we wanted to, whereas Joy seemed unable to do so. Sometimes she would giggle herself into exhaustion, by which time no one else thought it funny.

Then about a month after Cheryl died, when Joy was four, the paediatrician called at our home to see us. A short time into the visit Joy started to giggle. Even the doctor laughed at first, but when it continued I could see the look on the doctor's face change. Before she left she told us that these giggling fits were simply that – "fits" of epileptic activity over which Joy had no control.

Like Cheryl, Joy's seizures had started around the age of two, but this type of seizure was completely new to me. We were rather sad that this seemingly funny behaviour was in fact doing Joy's brain harm, and it was difficult to discourage Paul from doing anything that would make her laugh. He really did love making her laugh! Unfortunately this type of seizure was not easy to control, and so yet more medication was added to her daily regime, making her response slightly duller, but thankfully not stopping it altogether.

For the next few years things ticked along almost normally for us, with no major emergencies. However, Joy's problem with writhing muscles was made worse by jerking movements which could have her off your knee in a flash if you weren't holding on to her tightly! (The condition was described by her paediatrician as choreo-athetosis.) In essence it caused muscles inside the body to move in an unnatural fashion, like those in her limbs. One of the consequences of this was that Joy suffered similar stomach problems to those we had seen years earlier in Cheryl.

She had started to suffer from gastric reflux, which caused her pain, while at the same time she found swallowing difficult. Feeding her took a long time, and the effort she expended probably used up all the calories in the dish. She would cough and splutter throughout the whole exercise, and neither of us enjoyed the experience. Input from the speech therapist, physio, and new seating did nothing to help solve the problem, so when she was eight years old, Joy was admitted to hospital for an assessment of her feeding problems.

Thankfully, for all of our sakes, she wasn't admitted to the ward where Cheryl had died. A small twelve-bedded unit below the main hospital corridor, had been renovated to provide eight paediatric neurology beds, and a four-bedded dermatology ward. It was away from the bustle of the hospital, and was bright and welcoming. The best bit for me was that I really felt Joy was in the safe hands of staff who had experience in caring for children with complex needs. Our son was even more delighted to discover that the ward carried his name: Paul Ward! In the years to come, the staff there became almost like members of an extended family, while the side ward was affectionately referred to as Joy's second bedroom.

Joy's initial admission to Paul Ward was purely for observation and assessment. She was otherwise healthy, and I had checked that the ward was free of the bronchiolitis outbreak that was affecting other parts of the hospital at that time. I was reassured that Joy would not be at risk from this viral chest disease that was virtually guaranteed to close wards every year. It was an alarming condition that caused severe illness and even death in the very young and vulnerable. So Joy and I passed a rather boring week, with the occasional test being carried out, and various experts coming along and making suggestions to try to resolve her feeding problems.

A cup of tea was always a welcome break in the monotony, and as parents were allowed the use of the ward kitchen outside the children's mealtimes, it was often there that parents met one another and shared stories of their child's illness, and subsequent progress. I had noticed during the week that the side ward opposite the area where Joy was being nursed seemed to be cloaked in secrecy. The door was kept closed, and it was clear that the child inside was very ill. Those visitors who quietly moved in and out looked stressed and weary, at times with tear-stained faces. My heart went out to them all, as I knew exactly how they felt. So I prayed, asking God to heal their child.

One evening I was standing alone in the kitchen waiting for the kettle to boil, when another lady joined me. I recognized her as the mother of the child in the side ward. The atmosphere was very uncomfortable as we waited for the "watched kettle", so I decided to break the silence.

"I do hope your little one is improving… I have been praying for him."

My empathy for her broke the dam and her tears flowed. As I put my arm around this stranger's shoulders to try to offer comfort, I sensed the kind of despair that I knew only too well.

"You don't need to tell me anything," I quickly added, not wanting to intrude on private ground.

Yet sometimes conversing with a stranger can give you the freedom to say the things that might cause pain to those who are nearest to you. As I rattled a spoon in the big mug of tea that I had made for her, she opened her heart to me for a few short minutes. She went on to explain how her previously healthy two-year-old son had succumbed to bronchiolitis two weeks earlier. Her chin wobbled, and huge, hot tears once more brimmed over and rolled down her cheeks, as she related how he appeared to be losing his battle with this dreadful disease.

"The doctors don't think he's going to make it," she wept.

We stood together in silence for a few short seconds – two mothers, strangers, yet companions on this journey, seeking health for our children. After she composed herself, we walked the short distance into the ward together. I never saw her again. When I returned to the ward early the next morning, the side ward was empty.

Fear now took up residence alongside sadness as I thought of that little boy. Over a week earlier we had been told that there was no bronchiolitis in Paul Ward, yet that was evidently not the case. But for now I decided to keep my concerns to myself.

Feeding Joy that lunchtime was more difficult than usual. She was choking and spluttering, and all within view of the paediatrician who was providing weekend cover for the ward. When the doctor had finished with the child she had come to see, she approached us with a disturbed look on her face.

"Why is… *this child*… not being tube fed?" she asked as she searched for Joy's name on the sign above her bed.

I was rather shocked at her interference, as she wasn't Joy's doctor, but replied that I wanted to keep things as normal as possible for Joy.

"I would really prefer not to go down the road of artificial feeding," was my final remark.

"I would certainly not call *this* 'normal'!" she said, waving her hand at Joy's poor attempts at swallowing.

As she left the room, I felt humiliated and perplexed. Of course the doctor was right in her assessment of what she had observed – up to a point.

"Why did she have to watch you today, Joy?" I

moaned. "What's up, honey?" I queried as I lifted her out of her chair. "You're just not yourself this morning."

Then as I went to tuck in her clothes, my hands touched her bare back and I gasped.

"You're burning up, Joy!"

Five hours later, after X-rays, examinations and physiotherapy to obtain samples from her lungs, Joy was worse. In fact she looked very sick indeed. The ward sister came and sat down beside me with a look that told me all was not well.

"Catherine, we will have to move Joy into the side ward," she said sheepishly. "The doctors are afraid that she might have bronchiolitis."

As she started to prepare for the move I could contain my frustration no longer.

"Why was I told, over a week ago, that there was no bronchiolitis in the ward, when that little boy in the side ward had it?"

Sister knew the excuses she presented were feeble in the light of Joy's condition, and she also realized that what Joy was suffering from was hospital-acquired.

To make matters worse, when the on-call paediatrician returned, she requested that we allow Joy to be tube fed, as our child no longer had the energy required to feed by mouth. So Joy experienced tubes, and drips and oxygen for the first time. And my heart sank.

"Is this where it starts, Lord?" I whispered, as a sense of déjà vu gripped my heart.

The next few weeks were nightmarish, as Joy's condition deteriorated because she was exposed to yet another, but more serious, hospital-acquired infection. This organism went on to colonize her lungs, only to flare up at regular intervals and become a most serious cause of lung disease for Joy.

When we eventually left the hospital Joy was in a far worse condition than when she had entered it. Instead of our wriggly, giggly Joy we took home a sick, weak child who required fairly intensive nursing. Tube-feeding, inhaled medication, and also suctioning to help keep her lungs clear became part of her new daily routine. Deep down I knew we had stepped on to the roller coaster once again, and I wasn't looking forward to the ride.

Paul was now a teenager, and starting to see the unfairness of life more clearly. His little sister stayed quite little, as she continued to lose weight. Her days were often plagued by sickness, but he continued to tenderly slip her on to his knee and read to her from her "noisy" books. The smiles came less easily now, but if anyone could draw them from her, it was Paul. We never had any doubt that Joy recognized Paul's voice. Now and then, all three of us would talk about Heaven, but it was less often than before. Instead Paul became good at sorting out the various pieces of equipment that Joy needed, and making sure his mum was all right, especially when his dad was away preaching. He was learning to take on a protector's role far too early in his life.

Joy's difficulties were sharply contrasted by Paul's blossoming musical talent. Music was in his blood (well, on the Campbell side anyway!) and he seemed to excel at everything he put his hand to. Music festivals and school concerts were a great diversion, and we loved the chance to encourage him whenever we could. His teenage years were a breeze, and for that we thank God. Even the staff on Paul Ward loved to catch up with all that he was doing when he came to visit Joy during her many admissions.

Whereas Cheryl's last few years had been spent, for the most part, quietly sleeping, Joy's were dreadful. She slept only for very short periods, and appeared to be in a lot of pain. In time the vomiting problem was making her life a misery, with fears that it could also be adding to her breathing difficulties. So in 1997, after much discussion, we reluctantly agreed to gastric surgery, in order "to give Joy some quality of life, for whatever time she has left," as the surgeon had put it.

Sitting in the ward, we became anxious as Joy's time in theatre went long past what we were told to expect. Eventually we sighed with relief as the surgeon came towards us, still dressed in his theatre greens. Just as quickly we realized that he wasn't smiling.

"It's over!" he said, and we waited for the "but".

"But the surgery was much more difficult than I expected," he continued, trying to explain what had happened. "Joy bled a lot in theatre. We've managed to stop the bleeding. The staff from Intensive Care will send for you when they get her settled."

His look of exhaustion matched our look of anxious disappointment.

"Intensive care!"

A little wave of panic swept over me, as the enemy of my soul teased me with the suggestion that perhaps surgery was the wrong decision after all. Seeing Joy later in ICU did nothing to dispel those doubts, and for Philip it was one of the worst moments of his life.

Joy's recovery was hampered by one complication after another, and I longed day after day to take her home, to escape somehow, and take her away from all this suffering. At times we can equate a place with a problem. For example, Joy was in Paul Ward, and therefore I felt it was the ward's fault that she was so ill – so if I could take her home, then she would be OK. My thinking was totally illogical, but the staff understood that the more ill Joy became, the more I wanted to take her home. Eventually both sides came to realize that my problem was that I didn't want Joy's death to be like Cheryl's. I really wanted Joy to die at home. So after discussions with her paediatrician, I was promised that if at all possible, I would be able to take Joy home when the time came. It brought some degree of peace.

Early on 28 July 1997 I slipped into the ward to discover that I wasn't the only one with secret plans for the day. A silver banner was already attached across the top of the side-ward door, announcing: "Happy Birthday" to Joy! Inside, two of my favourite nurses were just finishing dressing her in the birthday dress I had left for her the night before. They had come in early that morning in order to have her ready before I arrived. Bright ribbons draped her cot, and a little pile of presents and cards was already sitting on the bedcover.

Philip and Paul joined the celebrations soon afterwards, and some of Paul's masterpieces were added to the decorations. All day staff from other departments who knew Joy called in to see her, and as family and friends swelled the numbers too, Joy's little side ward was buzzing with laughter and happy chatter. She was twelve years old that day, but had remained small enough to be cuddled and held, looking more like a toddler than nearly a teenager. However, the big badge that her brother pinned to her dress proudly declared every one of those twelve years. And although she didn't get to taste the cake baked for her in the hospital kitchen, all of her visitors did. It was truly a wonderful birthday!

Thankfully, not long after her birthday we were able to take her home once again.

13

On Butterfly Wings

Unfortunately, due to the complications that arose during her surgery, Joy did not regain any improvement in her quality of life. Instead, she had merely exchanged one form of discomfort for another. Her nutrition was now more severely compromised than ever, thereby further lowering her resistance to infection. Early in December that year Joy was back in hospital for what we thought would be her last time. Family and friends rallied with their support and prayers once more, as they had been doing faithfully for our family over a period totalling some eighteen years.

Watching Joy suffer on a daily basis was difficult for us all. Philip was trying to continue in his ministry as an itinerant evangelist, yet he found it increasingly difficult to be away from home. He had started to carry a small pager with him to ensure he could be contacted quickly if necessary. Meanwhile, Paul was in the middle of studying for his GCSE examinations. I was therefore the one who spent most of the time at the hospital, and I was starting to feel the old pangs of anger and resentment grow again as I watched the precious baby of our family suffer.

"Why does it have to be this way, Lord?" I would question. "All this suffering is so unfair!"

Yet I dreaded becoming bitter and despairing as I had before, so I asked God to set a guard on my heart.

"Help me to *choose* acceptance," I would plead. "Help me to trust You with what I can't understand, Lord."

Slowly I began to realize that the darkest time Joy would have to go through would provide her with the brightest of all rainbows – the promise of Heaven. That rainbow held the promise of no tears, no more pain, no sorrow, no more death – for ever. And the ultimate joy: God Himself will be with us! (See Revelation 21.)

During the times when she was distressed, I would hold her close and tell her that it would soon be over, singing to her every song I knew about Heaven. I read about Heaven, and I thought about Heaven, and I sang about Heaven, until its very brightness started to break up the blackness of despair in my soul.

But Joy did survive that Christmas, and although from that time onwards she required oxygen and monitoring, and occasional blood transfusions on top of everything else, I knew she had been spared for a purpose. In the following February the Children's Hospice Project was launched, and Joy (along with other children) helped spearhead that campaign. God had given our brave little girl one more job to do before allowing her to stand under her final rainbow.

"I've got her bedroom ready for her, Catherine," the staff nurse said over the phone. "The paediatrician told us you were on your way, so just come on in as soon as you can."

As we drove to the hospital I reckoned that almost fifteen months had passed since that dreadful Christmas when we were expecting Joy to leave us. She was now a teenager, a thought I didn't like, because the term almost mocked the slip of a little girl that she was. Spring was just around the corner, and the days had started to stretch.

Hope for the earth was on its way for another year, another season when life would shoot from the ground once more.

But Joy's condition was not showing the same signs of renewed vigour. Instead she was very ill once again. This time her bowel had stopped working, which had led to a small part of her lower left lung collapsing.

It was down to waiting time again.

The doctor had already explained to us that Joy's organs were starting to give up, as she had now entered what was referred to medically as "the terminal phase" of her condition.

A few days later it was Mother's Day (14 March 1999), and Philip was due to come and relieve me at the ward, as I had been booked to speak at a ladies' church service on behalf of the Children's Hospice Appeal. I lifted Joy out of her cot to dress her, but her breathing became distressed. Feeling that I couldn't leave her, I sent Philip to the service instead. By the time he had returned to be with us, I had made up my mind that it was time to bring Joy home. Philip agreed. There was nothing more anybody could do for our sweet child, and we wanted her to be at home with all the family. As we walked back from lunch we decided that we would talk to Paul about it later, and ask the doctor for permission to take Joy home the next day.

Chest physiotherapy can appear quite brutal sometimes, and Paul arrived with his granny just as the physio (whom we knew very well) was doing her "stuff". Joy rarely got upset with this procedure, as she was so used to it, but on this occasion a slight moan was heard as her chest was pummelled. Paul, now seventeen, seemed to sense immediately that Joy was very unwell, and as he watched, he suddenly caught the physio's arm and shouted at her.

"Why don't you leave her alone!" he yelled. "Can't you see that you're hurting her?"

"Paul!" I exclaimed, startled at this uncharacteristic outburst.

With that he ran out of the room, with Granny in close pursuit.

"Let him be, Catherine," said the physio, as I tried to apologize. "He's just upset," she remarked, with an understanding look. "He can see how sick Joy is, and he's only trying to protect her."

Reassurance rather than rebuke was what Paul needed, I thought, as I realized that the physio's comments were correct. Paul was anxious and embarrassed when he rejoined us. Trying to cover it up, he took out a parcel and placed it under Joy's arm.

"Happy Mother's Day, Mum – from both of us!"

With hugs and jokes we tried to lighten the atmosphere, and I also got the chance to kiss my own mother, thanking her for loving all of us. Joy was too weak to be held, and dozed off after an exhausting afternoon.

Soon the room was quiet again, and I sat for a few minutes enjoying the silence before walking down to the ward kitchen to fill the kettle. It was a slow old thing, so I came back to fetch the dish of pasta my mum had brought in for my tea.

"Time you went over on your side, Sweetheart," I said to the still sleeping Joy, as I slid my arms under her and turned her from her back to rest on her right side.

Almost immediately the alarm on the oxygen monitor went off, creating a loud noise. I looked to see if I had knocked off the probe when I had turned her over, but no, it was still in place. Glancing at Joy I could see that she was struggling to breathe. Immediately I reached for the oxygen valve and turned it up, quickly returning her to her previous position on her back. The alarm was displaying a very low level of oxygen saturation in her blood. Her breathing was fast, her lips grey, and the alarm was still screaming.

"Why have none of the girls come? Can't they hear the noise?" I ran out of the room shouting "Nurse!"

Immediately the nurses sprang into action, one going for a doctor while the other worked with the oxygen and Joy, trying to get both into harmony again.

After about ten minutes the crisis was over. Joy's oxygen level had improved, but she groaned pathetically when the doctor was listening to her chest.

"Poor Joy," the doctor said to her tenderly, "you are having a bad day! We'll just take a picture of your chest and see what's going on."

I loved it when the medics spoke to Joy personally. I knew the comments were really for me, but I liked it when they treated her as a little individual in her own right.

The pasta had been "zapped" in the microwave and I had just settled down to eat it when the doctor returned with the X-ray. She held it against the light and pointed to one side of the large film.

"It's not good," she said with a deep sigh. "The remainder of Joy's left lung has collapsed. She's only working on one lung now, Catherine."

I didn't flinch, as my protection mechanism went into operation. No tears, no panic – nothing! I felt nothing. I said nothing. The doctor cleared her throat, the small noise breaking the silence.

"I've spoken to the on-call consultant," she continued. "He says if you would like to take Joy home, you can."

Still I didn't speak. I just reached forward and held Joy's hand, while an inner voice said, "I will be with you."

My mind was in a whirl, and the doctor sounded far

away, but I could just about hear the final words of the little speech she had carefully prepared before entering the room.

"If her oxygen level drops again, it's unlikely she will survive – do you understand what I am saying?"

She seemed to sense that I wasn't quite with her, so she raised her voice to obtain the necessary effect.

"I've heard it all before," I replied, in a manner that must have sounded a bit rude, as I tried to decide whether things really were that bad.

"Catherine, Joy has never been this ill before. I don't think she'll see the morning." With that she turned to go.

"I'm sorry," I said, stopping her for a few short seconds, as quiet tears at last started to fall. "I'll speak to my husband about taking Joy home. We would really like that."

It was hard for the girls in the ward to help me pack up Joy's things. They even filled a carrier bag with medication and supplies, just in case Joy proved them all wrong yet again. Then each of them in turn kissed her goodbye, knowing it would be the last time they would see their wriggly, giggly Joy.

By ten o'clock that night Joy was tucked up snugly in bed in her own room at home. Unfortunately, we had had very little time to prepare Paul for the sudden decision that was forced on us because of Joy's rapid deterioration. When we arrived home he was agitated and confused.

"Why have you done this, Mum? If Joy is so ill, why have you brought her home?" he questioned, as he sat on her bedroom floor while I was sorting things out.

I sensed that somehow he thought this was some mad scheme that his mother had dreamed up, and that because of it we were putting Joy in danger. Stopping what I was doing, I sat on the bed facing Paul, who was clearly hurting.

"Son, Joy is *dying*. The doctor has said that she can either die in hospital or die at home with us. Which do you think is better for Joy... and for all of us?"

It was an awful question for a seventeen-year-old to contemplate. I pulled him off the floor where he sat in silence, with his lip quivering, and I held him close. As my grip relaxed he pulled back.

"Here, of course... but it's not fair, Mummy... none of this is fair!"

And he was right.

Amazingly, Joy was not only settled in her own bed, but her oxygen level and pulse had all returned to normal levels. It confirmed to me that we had done the right thing in bringing her home, as I watched her sleeping peacefully under the dim light of the bedside lamp. Because she was so settled, and our bedroom was literally only feet away, we stretched out and dozed lightly, checking her frequently throughout the night.

Suddenly, in the early hours of the morning, the alarm from the oxygen monitor squealed at us from her room, and we both raced in to see the figures slowly falling. I tried to waken Joy, without wanting to frighten her, while Philip changed the oxygen cylinder that was registering low. His hands shook as he tried to hurry the process, but turning up the new cylinder to a higher rate made no difference.

It was happening – the moment we were all dreading. Joy was dying.

"Quickly, Philip!" I shouted. "Go and phone our parents – maybe they'll get here in time!"

As he ran to the phone, I rushed into Paul's room. He was just stirring with all the noise, and as calmly as I could, I told him that Joy was going fast.

"It's up to you, Son. If you want to be with her, you need to come now. If you don't, we'll come and tell you when it's over. The choice is yours – I can't make it for you."

I felt so very guilty as I left his room: guilty that I had caused him so much pain, and guilty that he had to make choices that he would have to live with the rest of his life.

"O God, please give us the grace to get through this!" I cried from my heart.

As I sat at the top of Joy's bed with my arm around her shoulder, Philip sat further down the bed holding her hand. Soon Paul joined us, and reached forward to turn the sound off on the monitor. He sat on the floor in silence. There was a strange sense of peace in the room. God was fulfilling His promise once more, because each of us knew that He was there with us. There was no panic, only silent tears, as we talked to Joy of the lovely place she was going to.

"Don't be afraid, Sweetheart," I said, gently planting a kiss on her forehead.

When I lifted my head again, the light from the lamp was shining through the silk butterfly that was clipped to it. In a flash, God gave me a beautiful picture of what was happening to our daughter at that very moment. Just as the butterfly breaks through its chrysalis, leaving its old earth-bound shell behind to soar into the sky, so Joy was leaving behind her old, twisted and pain-filled body to take on her new heavenly body, which would allow *her* to soar as she had never done before.

"Joy," I exclaimed, "look at the butterfly, Pet. You are getting a new body, right now, Sweetheart! Soon you are going to fly, like the butterfly, straight to Heaven!"

She moaned as if distressed, and I told her it was OK

to go – that Jesus was waiting – that we would be all right.

As the numbers on the monitor plummeted to zero, we each kissed our beautiful, brave Joy goodbye, heartbroken at our loss, yet heartened by the picture that helped to ease our pain. Joy was now perfect, and for the first time she was soaring! It was 5 a.m. on 15 March 1999.

If a death can ever be described as a "good" death, then Joy's was. She died at home surrounded by those who loved her, assured that her suffering was over, now with only freedom and perfection ahead. Heartache was undoubtedly revisited, on many occasions, but not despair. I had left that at the Cross a number of years earlier. I had also learned since then that peace lies in acceptance – the type of acceptance that rests on the knowledge that God knows what He is doing even when we don't; the type of acceptance that acts on that knowledge and lives each day by faith. That kind of acceptance brings freedom.

Even Joy's funeral was different.

It was sad, yes, but also triumphant as the large congregation listened to Philip bravely pay his own remarkable tribute to his little girl, as his last act of fatherly love. The whole congregation watched as he made his way to the pulpit; each person present wondering where he would get the strength to speak while a little white coffin stood only feet away from him. But he did speak, his words addressed to our beautiful daughter whose remains were about to leave us.

"Our dear Joy," he began.

> *Today our church is filled with people who want*
> *to remember you and give thanks to God for the*
> *remarkable little girl that you were. Your mum and*

I felt it right to make our own tribute to you today, for nobody knew you better than we did.

The day you were born – 28 July 1985 – our whole family rejoiced; how could we have called you anything else but "Joy"? From that day on, the sunshine of your smile lit up our home and our lives. True, we were all saddened when we discovered that – like your sister Cheryl before you – your little head showed that you too had microcephaly. We knew then exactly the kind of problems that lay ahead… but you just kept on smiling.

And there were lots of smiles during your short life of thirteen and a half years – probably more than people might think. For one thing, quite apart from the time when you were the centre of attention, surrounded by a family who adored you, there were many happy days in Lillian Hill's class at Hillcroft School. When the bus came for you each morning, we knew that both you and your friends would be superbly looked after by the wonderful staff there. Hillcroft was, and is, a very special place.

Of course, there was another special place you visited far too often: Paul Ward at the Royal Belfast Hospital for Sick Children. The side ward there became almost like your second bedroom, but the nurses who cared for you there were brilliant, weren't they? And your consultant, Dr Elaine Hicks, always made sure you had the best of attention and the finest possible treatment. Dr Hicks is a Paediatric Neurologist and a very clever lady, but even she was constantly baffled by how you kept bouncing back after so many bouts of serious illness.

But I suppose we shouldn't really have been
surprised. The care you received in Paul Ward was
unfailingly first class; your mum was always there
to look after you; and so many people were praying
for you that God – Who loves you more than we
ever could – just kept on answering those prayers.
It was while you were in hospital in December
1997 that it seemed your time with us was about
to come to an end, but again you pulled through,
surprising us all once more. You were spared to us
for another fifteen months, and it does seem to us
that was for a purpose.

When Tom Hill had the vision to build the first
children's hospice in Northern Ireland, he thought of
using your story to help people realize how much it
was needed and how it could help families like ours.
Of course, hospices aren't needed where you are
now, but maybe your contribution will help set up
a service which many life-limited children and their
families will be able to use and enjoy.

As Philip continued, my heart swelled with pride, both
for the little girl who had departed and her amazing father
who spoke about her so eloquently.

You know, Joy, even though you couldn't walk or
talk, read or write, run or play, your life has touched
lots of people – just look at how many are here
today – and your mum and I have certainly learned
important lessons from you. You showed us how
to be brave in the face of suffering. We know only
too well the many uncomfortable and often painful
experiences you had to go through down the years.
Not long ago, you were even recognized as a "Child

of Courage" – but we already knew that.

    You also opened many doors for us, especially into the lives of families with children who have problems like yours. Your little life became like a bridge to many hearts and many homes. And through it all, we have learned again that "God makes no mistakes". In spite of what some might think, your life had worth and value way beyond your limitations, and our family is left much the poorer because you are no longer with us.

    Life without you is not going to be easy. We have loved you for more than thirteen years and we aren't going to stop now. But as we make difficult adjustments to our daily lives, how glad we are to have a super family and some wonderful friends – all of whom will be praying for us. But best of all is the Friend we have in Jesus, and we can be sure that He will never leave us nor forsake us.

    The lamp beside your bed has a model of a butterfly clinging to it, and what has just happened to you has reminded us that, just as a butterfly breaks free of its chrysalis to take wings and fly, so you have been released to enjoy a whole new life with God in Heaven. In the Bible, Paul writes about how he wanted to be "absent from the body and present with the Lord". You'll not be sorry to be "absent" from your little body: it didn't work very well, and often it was sick and weak. But if we could see you now, free of handicaps, chest infections and epilepsy, how could we possibly wish you back? Best of all, you're now "present with the Lord" and – as Paul also said – that is "far better".

    Many people have loved and cared for you down the years – apart from those we have already

mentioned at Hillcroft and in Paul Ward – and
it would take too long to mention them all. But
we have to say that we have been blessed with
a wonderful family. How could we ever have
managed without the help of your grannies and
grandas, the love and support of your aunties,
uncles and little cousins. Paul has always been
your devoted, caring big brother, and he will miss
you as much as we will.

Lots of people have called at our home in the
last few days, and others have telephoned to say they
were thinking about us. Did you know we have had
calls from as far away as Canada and Bolivia? Still
others have sent cards and letters. I know you would
want us to say "thank you" to them all.

Just yesterday a letter arrived from a captain
in the Salvation Army, and in it he told us of a little
girl he knew who had many of the same problems
you had. What he said about her we could truthfully
say about you:

"She never spoke, maybe could not see and
it was doubtful she could hear. Yet she managed
to achieve something I have never managed in a
lifetime. Her unique role was to bring the best out
of other people. Even the more hard-bitten would
soften with her. She never had a bad word for
anyone; she never had an argument; she never (as
far as I am aware) committed a sin. I would have
been proud to have her as my daughter."

Darling Joy, we are so proud of you, and your
mum and I thank God for the privilege of having
been your parents.

Early on Monday morning you fell asleep in
your own bed, and opened your eyes in Heaven. You

*must have received quite a welcome up there – and
we know you'll have one ready for us when we see
you again. And it won't be very long till then, my
pet, it won't be long.*

Paul sat beside me, squeezing my hand as he watched his
dad with pride. Later on that beautiful spring day they
both carried Joy's coffin with the same pride. And the
wings of the wildflower butterfly wreath sitting on her
coffin seemed to flutter in the light breeze, reminding me
that Joy wasn't earthbound any more!

Just over a year later, I was standing at the kitchen sink
in the manse we had recently moved to in Coleraine,
when Paul's little blue car drove into the yard. I smiled
as he rushed out of the car, obviously very excited about
something. Picking up the towel to dry my hands as he ran
through the door, I didn't even get a chance to say hello.
Instead, he caught me in his arms and twirled me around.

"Mum, you should see it!"

"See what?" I replied, rather puzzled.

"The Children's Hospice!" he retorted, as if I should
have known what he was talking about. "I was driving up
the motorway and… you should see it, Mum. The walls
are so high now – it's amazing!" he said, hardly stopping
for breath. "But you know what's the best bit, Mum? Joy
is in every brick!"

And I basked in the pride of the moment.

For a period of almost twenty years, God had allowed me
to care for our two beautiful, brave daughters. I have never
stopped being their mother: it is just that now we cannot
be together for a while. They, however, continue to bless
my life every day that I live. I would be lying if I said that

I wouldn't have changed a thing, for what mother would deliberately choose suffering for her children? What I wouldn't change, however, is the perspective that having Cheryl and Joy has added to my thinking. I can now value people for who they are, and not merely for what they can do. And I am utterly convinced that life here pales into insignificance in comparison with what lies ahead for those who love Christ. Neither would I have wanted to miss all that I have learned about God, and from God. It has been both priceless and precious.

I have discovered that God is no man's debtor. He doesn't owe me anything, yet He continues to lavish His goodness upon me. Take Cheryl's twenty-sixth birthday, for instance. On that day God sent another blue-eyed blonde into our lives, in the form of Susie, Paul's new bride. God in His mercy is once more allowing me to enjoy the blessings of a daughter.

There is no doubt that many of my days have been storm-filled, but if they hadn't been, then I wouldn't have got to stand *Under the Rainbow*, and experience the unfailing promises of God.

For that I give God thanks.

Postscript

It had seemed such a long time since the bleep of a text message had wakened us in the middle of the night.

"Sorry for waking you – Susie has just been moved to the delivery suite ☺ Pray! Paul x"

And pray we did, for we could settle to nothing else. Only a few short messages came through in what turned out to be a very long day. Now sitting in my parents' home I was starting to become anxious. My old midwifery thinking cap was working overtime. Every now and then we bowed our heads and prayed for God's protection on both mother and baby.

"It's going to be a girl," my father suddenly announced, a wide grin on his face.

"A girl!" I replied. "That's something new from you. I thought no one else was allowed to have a girl since Cheryl and Joy?"

Every time one of his own children was expecting a baby my dad would quietly tell Mum that he hoped it wasn't a girl – he didn't want any other girls, not when he loved Cheryl and Joy so much. Amazingly he had five other grandchildren and every one of them was a boy!

"But it's OK now," he said, shrugging his shoulders. "It's going to be a girl – I just know it."

"Whatever it is, I wish he or she would hurry up… this isn't good for my heart!"

Now, close to 11 p.m. I could wait no longer, and

picked up the phone.

"I'll let your son speak to you himself," the midwife said in response to my inquiry.

"Hi Mum," came the familiar voice on the other end of the line. "I was just about to ring you… it's a girl!"

"A girl! Oh, Paul, that's wonderful."

By this time whoops of delight filled my parents' small sitting room.

"Mum, are you listening?" Paul continued as I shushed the happy throng. "We have a name picked. We're going to call her Bethany Joy."

I was speechless for a very few seconds, overwhelmed by the emotion of it all.

"Mum? Do you like it?"

"I love it, Son… thank you… and give our love to both of them. Can't wait to see you all. I love you."

And so Bethany Joy has come into our lives, more precious than anyone could ever imagine. God is so good. He gives, and gives, and gives again!

She is now a happy, bubbly toddler, filling our lives with joy and hope for the future. Recently, during a family visit, we were all busy chatting at the table while Bethany was still nibbling away at her food. Suddenly I heard her whisper my name.

"What did you say, sweetheart? Granny didn't hear you."

With her head cocked cutely to the side and a twinkle in her eye she simply replied, "Ganny, I love you."

What more could I wish for than that?